Samanūdi
Tajwīd Qā'ida For beginners

Abū Ādam Akhlāq
Dārul Qurrā' & Islamic Research Centre

القاعدة السمنودية

للمبتدئين

تأليف

أبو أدم محمد أخلاق الأزهري

قدَّم له

فضيلة الشيخ العلامة إبراهيم عبد الحميد آل المعلم السمنودي

SAMANUDI
PUBLICATIONS

وعن أبي هريرة رضى الله عنه أن رسول الله ﷺ قال:

... مَنْ غَشَّ فَلَيْسَ مِنَّا رواه الترمزى

Abu Hurairah ﷺ narrated that the Messenger of Allāh ﷺ said :
"Who so ever cheats, is not from amongst us"

Copyright © Samanudi Publications, 2022
First Edition 2022

Published by

Samanudi Publications
26 Oakwood Road
Birmingham
United Kingdom B4 11HA

00201558482555 - Egypt
00447411940950 - United Kingdom
abuadamakhlaq@gmail.com
www.samanudipublications.com
www.darulqurra.org

ISBN 978-1-73-923640-3

@DARULQURRAIRC

Type setting and page design by Abu Adam Akhlaq
Cover design by Manal Khalifa - Egypt
(manalkhalifastudio@gmail.com)

ISBN 978-1-73-923640-3

SAMANUDI
PUBLICATIONS

SCAN ME

darulqurra.org

حَدَّثَنَا هَنَّادٌ حَدَّثَنَا أَبُو مُعَاوِيَةَ عَنِ ابْنِ أَبِي لَيْلَى وَحَدَّثَنَا سُفْيَانُ بْنُ وَكِيعٍ

حَدَّثَنَا حُمَيْدُ بْنُ عَبْدِ الرَّحْمَنِ الرُّؤَاسِيُّ عَنِ ابْنِ أَبِي لَيْلَى عَنْ عَطِيَّةَ عَنْ أَبِي سَعِيدٍ قَالَ

قَالَ رَسُولُ اللَّهِ ﷺ

مَنْ لَمْ يَشْكُرِ النَّاسَ لَمْ يَشْكُرِ اللَّهَ

وَفِي الْبَابِ عَنْ أَبِي هُرَيْرَةَ وَالْأَشْعَثِ بْنِ قَيْسٍ وَالنُّعْمَانِ بْنِ بَشِيرٍ . قَالَ أَبُو عِيسَى هَذَا حَدِيثٌ حَسَنٌ صَحِيحٌ

Abu Hurairah ﷺ narrated that the Messenger of Allāh ﷺ said :

"Whoever is not thankful to the people,
he is not thankful to Allāh."

Darul Qurra
& ISLAMIC RESEARCH CENTRE

🐦@DarulQurra   f /DarulQurra

Darul Qurrā' & Islamic Research Centre sincerely appreciates the
continuous assistance and support from Jamia Al Karam, The World
Association for Al-Azhar Graduates (WAAG), Samanudi Publications,
City Law Chambers, Pro Accountancy Luton, Millat Auto Spares LTD
and AA Carpets.

Name of Learner

Name of Tutor

Start Date			Completion Date		
Day	Month	Year	Day	Month	Year
Signed by tutor			Signed by tutor		

SAMANUDI
PUBLICATIONS

المقدمة

بسم الله الرحمن الرحيم

بسم الله الرحمن الرحيم

الحمد لله الذي أعظم مِنّ عباده بِسِرّ ... كتابه والصلاة والسلام على نبينا محمد صلى الله عليه وسلم الذي نزل عليه تقريءٌ لروح الأمين بكتابٍ مبين الذي جعله الله أفضل الأذكار تقرباً لله ورفعه به ذكرًا ... وذكرًا ... الأمر إلى يوم الدين وقد أمر الله نبيه محمد صلى الله عليه وسلم أن يقرأ القرآن ملك لناس على مكث فقام ... لناس وعمر لحودِتيه لهذا الكتاب قراءة وصوتًا ... كأنه ... ولقد جعل الله ... في دوامٍ لكتابه الله تعالى وتلاوته وما يزال القرآن يقرأ لِحُظّاظِه ... في زمانِنا هذا وقد جعل العلماء لهذا الكتاب قواعد منظومات ...

فأقول أنا الشيخ / إبراهيم المعلم الذي قرأ القرآن على شيخ مسعود بابضغرى ... ...

فضيلة الشيخ العلامة / إبراهيم بن عبدالحميد بن إبراهيم آل المعلم

القارئ بالقراءات العشر المتواترة
وعضو مشيخة المقارئ المصرية
والمدرس السابق بمعاهد القراءات بمصر
والمدرس السابق للقران وعلومه بالأزهر الشريف

١٠ ربيع الاول ١٤٤٤هجري

الشيخ
أبراهيم عبد الحميد آل المعلم
مدرس القرآن وعلومه
بالأزهر الشريف

Foreward
(Abbreviated translation)

Allāh's name we begin with, the Most Gracious, the Most Merciful.

Praise be to Allāh ﷻ who chose from His entire creation, the one who He gifted His Book. Peace and infinite blessings be upon our Prophet Muhammad ﷺ upon whom the trustworthy Jibrāīl ﷺ descended with this clear Book Qur'ān, from which He made the best of His remembrances for His closeness, and the remembrance of His Prophet ﷺ and the remembrance of his nation among all nations until the Day of Judgment.

Allāh ﷻ commanded his Prophet Muhammad ﷺ to recite the Qur'ān to his companions, who then continued to recite to those who followed and they were the best of us who preserved this book in its correct reading with rules (Tajwīd) and performance.

I, (Shaykh) / Ibrāhīm Āle Al Mualim who read the Qur'ān to Sheikh ul Qurrā, Imām Ibrāhīm Alī Shehāta Al-Samanūdī in the ten minor and the major Qirā`āt, ask Allāh to bless Ustādh Abū Ādam Muhammad Akhlāq for what he has presented to us that will certainly benefit students with correct recitation and memorisation of the Qur'ān and its Qirā'āt at Darul Qurra in United Kingdom, Egypt and other Places. Students will gain understanding just as he attained the understanding of the ten minor and major Qirā'āt with Ijāza from Samanūd, and this is a great deed for which the reward is only with Allāh.

The Messenger of Allāh ﷺ highlighted that the best among you is the one who learns the Qur'ān and teaches it. Whoever follows this path in seeking and serving knowledge, Allāh will make it easy for him the path to heaven. The first command given to the Messenger of Allāh ﷺ when he met with angel Jibrāīl ﷺ was to 'Read', because it is only by reading and memorising the Qur'ān with which we can gain honour and status. May your parents wear the crown of jewellery and light, may Allāh ﷻ reward and bless our teachers and leaders with goodness on our behalf as they transmitted the Qur'ān so sweetly and beatifully with emmense generosity. This is what we ask for Sheikh Mohammed (Abu Adam Akhlāq), Umar Akhlāq, Ali Akhlāq and Mikhaael Māla that Allāh ﷻ bless them the crown of dignity on the Day of Resurrection and may Allāh ﷻ reward learners with the best.

Honourable Sheykh, Ibrāhīm bin Abdul Ḥamīd bin Ibrāhīm Āle Al Mua'lim

Reciter of all the famous and mass transmitted Qirā'āt
Member of the Mashaykhah Al-Maqāri' Al-Masriyyah
Retired Lecturer of Faculty of Qirā'āt Egypt
Retired Lecturer of Qur'ān & Sciences at Al-Azhar Al-Sharīf

10 Rabi Al Awwal 1444 Hijrī

Foreward

All praise is for Allāh, Lord of all the worlds. Prayers of peace and blessings be upon the final Messenger Muhammad ﷺ and his family and companions.

The Qur'an, the final revelation from Allāh Almighty, was revealed in the Arabic Language spoken by the Messenger of Islam, Prophet Muhammad ﷺ. Within a century after its revelation, Muslim conquests spanned over a territory ranging from Spain and Morocco in the West, to Transoxiana and Sind in the East, Yemen in the South, and bordering Armenia in the North. This laid the foundation of the Islamic civilisation which was founded upon the message of the Qur'an, thereby making its language highly significant throughout the realm and rendering it the first step towards any progress. Today Muslims are present all over the world who speak different languages, yet the Qur'an which bonds them all together ensures that learning the Arabic Language, more precisely the Qur'anic Arabic Language, continues to be the centre of their devotion and learning outcome.

Over the course of centuries, the Arabic language has passed through many phases, noticeably in its writing and script, and there have been many different approaches towards learning the language with its correct pronunciation and detail, and for learners of different ages, from young children to those beginners with differing mother tongues. Regional variances of the Indian subcontinent, the Middle East, and other continents of the world also play a part in having developed different techniques. The world today is much more connected than ever before resembling a global village, in which knowledge and various experiences are also coming together. As time moves on, the learners and indeed the tutors of today are much different too, compared to those in the near past, let alone the distant past.

The book in hand, the Samanudi Tajwīd Qāida, authored by the talented teacher and Qur'an reciter, Ustadh Abu Adam Muhammad Akhlaq al-Azhari, is indeed a new manual for learning and correctly pronouncing and reciting the language of the Qur'an. It presents a new methodology, distinguished from various predecessors, with a new approach in learning this science, especially of benefit for those wishing to pursue further intermediate and advanced texts in a steady and step-by-step manner. If not revolutionary, this book can surely be considered evolutionary.

With this context in mind, and in service of the Qur'an and its sublime language, it gives us great joy in recognising and appreciating the various literary and teaching projects undertaken by Darul Qurra & Islamic Research Centre in Birmingham, an initiative established by the learned brothers, Ustadh Abu Adam Muhammad Akhlaq al-Azhari and Maulana Zein Hud al-Azhari. Both being graduates of Jamia Al-Karam having furthered their respective studies in Egypt, the land of Al-Azhar Al-Sharif. No doubt, they are recipients of well-wishes and prayers from their teacher, Shaykh Muhammad Imdad Hussain Pirzada, the founder of Jamia Al-Karam.

In attributing this book to his teacher, Shaykh Allama Ibrahīm Shehāta al-Samanudi, the author has given due value to chains of transmission and knowledge, maintaining the etiquette that traditionally exists between teachers and students. I pray that Allāh Almighty grants this effort divine acceptance and blesses the author and those who support him with greater benevolence in both worlds. Amin.

Bakhtyar H Pirzada al-Azhari
Vice-Principal, Jamia Al-Karam
Vice-President, Al-Azhar Alumni UK

27th December 2022

Eaton Hall, Retford DN22 0PR, United Kingdom
mail: info@alkaram.org tel: 01777 706441

Acknowledgements

All praise is for Allāh ﷻ Lord of the universe, who has sent us Qur'an: The Sublime Word - through his Beloved Messenger, our Master ﷺ as a light and guidance. O Allāh ﷻ send infinite peace and blessings upon our Beloved Messenger ﷺ, his household, his companions and all those who follow.

Writing this book (Samanūdi Tajwīd Qāida for beginners) which I have named after my teacher, Sheikh ul Qurrā, Imām Ibrāhīm Alī Shehāta Al-Samanūdī ﵁ was certainly harder than I had expected, however I am hopeful in acceptance from Allāh. None of this would have been possible without the patience of my beloved wife, Umm Adam Akhlāq, who has always stood by me during my struggles and has allowed me to spend endless time with my teachers, countless nights writing and serving this beautiful science of Tajwīd.

I am eternally grateful to my honourable mentor and teacher Shaykh ul Qurrā', Imām Ibrāhīm Abdul Hamīd Al Mualim ﵀ from Samanūd, whom I have learnt great discipline, love, and knowledge that has helped me excel in the sciences of Qira'āt (*Al-'Ashara As-Sughra & Al-Kubra*). He was very patient and generous by allowing me to study, live and become part of his beautiful family. I truly have no idea on how to ever repay his generosity and kindness other than to ask Allāh ﷻ to shower His ﷻ infinite blessings upon his household and elevate his ranks in this life and the hereafter.

I would also like to take this opportunity to thank another great guide, mentor and teacher, Shaykh Imdād Hussain Pirzāda ﵀ founder and principal of Jāmia Al Karam where it all began for me as a young nine-year old child in 1995. After completing my secular studies by the age of sixteen, Shaykh Imdād Hussain Pirzāda ﵀ advised me to continue my Islamic education at Jāmia Al Karam and then to travel to the land of Al Azhar, Egypt, where i was blessed with the opportunity to sit and learn from hundreds of great Ulema. All of this would not have been possible if it was not for the great vision of Shaykh Imdād Hussain Pirzāda ﵀.

A very special thank you to my beloved brother Mājid Mahmūd of Citylaw Chambers of Luton to whom I am forever indebted to, for always standing and contributing to all projects of Dārul Qurrā & Islamic Research Centre, which we founded in 2013 to serve humankind around the world to reconnect with the essence and beauty of the Sublime Qur'ān. Mājid Mahmūd's advice and suggestions have played a pivotal role in developing the activities in this book which will undoubtably be of great benefit for generations to come. I ask Allāh ﷻ to shower endless blessings upon him and his family.

I am grateful to the ever patient friend, Yasir Rashid (Pro Accountancy - Luton) and Abid Hussain (AA Carpets - Luton) who have supported Dārul Qurrā wholeheartedly and have played an instrumental role in all its works.

I would also like to extend my deepest gratitude to Shaykh Mikhāīl Māla (Dārul Qurrā), Shaykh Mohammed Shu'ayr (Egypt), Imām 'Amār Hāfiz (Dārul Qurrā), Prof Claire Gallien (Zentrum für Islamische Theologie, Tübingen University), Dr Sahdia Akhlāq (Dārul Qurrā), Imam Sayyid Shoaib Shah (Stoke), Abu Isa Mohammed Yasin (Accrington) and the great designer, Manal Khalīfa (Egypt) who have played a decisive role in the completion of this book. From reading early drafts to giving me constructive advice on design so that I could complete this book to a very high standard.

Finally, I would like to express my deepest appreciation and acknowledgment to all my family, friends, colleagues and students for always being supportive of Dārul Qurrā & Islamic Research Centre. I thank you all for your support and help. I ask Allāh to shower His infinite blessings upon you all in this life and the hereafter.

Abu Adam Akhlāq Al Azhari
30th December 2022

بسم الله الرحمن الرحيم

ٱلَّذِى خَلَقَنِى فَهُوَ يَهْدِينِ ۝ وَٱلَّذِى هُوَ يُطْعِمُنِى وَيَسْقِينِ ۝ وَإِذَا مَرِضْتُ فَهُوَ يَشْفِينِ ۝ وَٱلَّذِى يُمِيتُنِى ثُمَّ يُحْيِينِ ۝ وَٱلَّذِى أَطْمَعُ أَن يَغْفِرَ لِى خَطِيٓئَتِى يَوْمَ ٱلدِّينِ ۝ رَبِّ هَبْ لِى حُكْمًا وَأَلْحِقْنِى بِٱلصَّٰلِحِينَ ۝ وَٱجْعَل لِّى لِسَانَ صِدْقٍ فِى ٱلْءَاخِرِينَ ۝ وَٱجْعَلْنِى مِن وَرَثَةِ جَنَّةِ ٱلنَّعِيمِ ۝ سورة الشعراء

صدق الله العظيم

Arabic language is spoken today by over 400 million people and is officially the national language of over 25 countries. Over the years, Arabic language has influenced many non-Arabic languages.

Arabic	English	Arabic	English
لَيِمُون	Lemon	قهوة	Coffee
أَلْجَبَر	Algebra	زرافة	Giraffe
قُطُن	Cotton	سفر	Safari
السُّكَّر	Sugar	قندي	Candy
غِيتَار	Guitar	غزال	Gazelle
كَرَفَان	Caravan	مطرح	Mattress
مَخْزَن	Magazine	الكحل	Alcohol
صُفَّة	Sofa	أمير	Admiral

Ka'b al-Aḥbār (died 32 AH) believed that the first person to coin the Arabic, Syriac and all other scripts was Prophet Ādam ﷺ. Three hundred years prior to his death, he wrote them on clay and baked them in fire. The clay tablets were later found after the earth recovered from the floods at the time of Prophet Nūh ﷺ.

Ibn 'Abbās ﷺ said that the origins of the Arabic script were laid down by Prophet Ismā'īl ﷺ.

Some scholars believe that a group of kings by the names of Abjad (ابجد), Hawwaz (هوز), Huttī (حطي), Kalamun (كلمن), Sa'afaṣ (سعفص), and Qarashat (قرشت) first came up with the script.

It is said that they coined the letters of the Arabic alphabet according to the letters in their names. The letters (ثخذضظغ) are not found in the names of the kings; hence, they were added afterwards to complete the Arabic alphabet. These additional letters are known as al-Rawādif.

Ibn Jinnī (died 392 AH) differed and wrote that the Arabic script was a derivative of another language called al-Musnad.

It has also been said that the origins of the script were established by Murāmir bin Murra, Aslam bin Sidra and 'Āmir ibn Jadara, who all lived in the ancient town of al Anbār in Iraq. They based it on the Syriac script.

Others have suggested that both, Syriac and Arabic, can be traced back to Aramaic, which was an ancient language spoken by Middle Eastern people known as Aramaeans.

Conclusion

It is clear from the above discussion that there is no certainty with regards to the exact origins of the Arabic script. In any case, pre-Islam Arab peninsula had commonly relied upon two types of scripts:

(i) *the ancient script of al-Musnad, which is referred to as the Southern   script.*

(ii) *the Northern script of Arabic, which is used in the Qur'an.*

Note: Al-Musnad became extinct just prior to Islam.

The original sequence of the Arabic alphabet was written in the Abjad format, which some believe to be the names of the six kings as discussed previously. The last six letters, which were added later to complete the Arabic alphabet, are not found in any other Semitic language.

Since they have been added to the end of the alphabet, they are called Al-Rawādif - 'the followers'. In the table below, they have been highlighted in blue.

Pre-Islamic Sequence of Arabic Language		
حطى	هوز	ابجد
ي ط ح	ز و هـ د	د ج ب ا
قرشت	سعفص	كلمن
ت ش ر ق	ص ف ع س	ن م ل ك
ضظغ		ثخذ
غ ظ ض		ذ خ ث

The Arabic script was modified to accommodate bedouins who spoke fluently but struggled to read and write Arabic. Non-Arabs who embraced Islam also struggled in learning to identify the letters that were written without dots and vowels.

To facilitate the bedouins and non-Arabs, Naṣr bin 'Āṣim (died 90 AH) grouped and arranged the Arabic alphabet based on the shape of the letters.

For example, since the letters Bā, Tā and Thā had a similar shape, they were grouped together. Likewise, Jīm, Hā and Khā were grouped together due to their similar shape. In the table below, the alphabet letters have been grouped according to their shapes.

Post-Islamic Sequence of Arabic Language

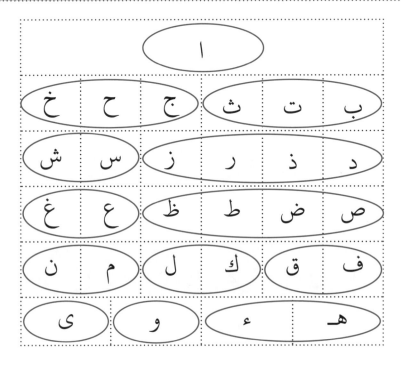

Today, there are more than twenty million Muslims in Europe with Germany and France leading with the largest Muslim populations. Western Muslims that are not familiar with arabic phonology struggle with learning the correct articulation (Tajwīd) of Arabic letters.

To overcome this challenge, we at Dārul Qurrā & Islamic Research Centre (Birmingham UK) have rearranged the letters of the Arabic alphabet in this book 'Samanūdī Tajwīd Qāida' based on their articulation points.

Revised Sequence of Arabic Language 21st Century

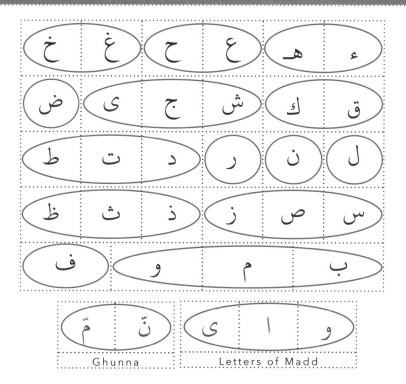

The Arabic script did not have dialectical vowels or dots in the pre-Islamic era. During the time of the Messenger of Allāh ﷺ, the Qur'ān was also memorised, written and preserved without dots and dialectical vowels.

Imam Abu 'Amr al Dāni (died 444 AH) explains:

Amīr Muāwiyah ؓ wrote to Ziyād ؓ asking for his son 'Ubayd-Allāh. When 'Ubayd arrived and spoke to Amīr Muāwiyah ؓ, he made many mistakes in the Arabic language. Amīr Muāwiya ؓ sent 'Ubayd back to his father Ziyād and wrote him a letter instructing him to admonish his son. He wrote, *"Reprimand 'Ubayd-Allāh! He is being wasted"*. So Ziyād sent a request to Abu Al-Aswad Al-Du'alī (died 69 AH), a student 'Alī ibn Abī Ṭālib ؓ saying:

> *'The Ḥamrā' (i.e. non-Arab tribes) have increased in number and have ruined the language of the Arabs. Can you compile something which people can use to mend their speech and vowelise the Book of Allāh?"*

Abu Al-Aswad Al-Du'alī rejected the request and expressed great dislike at the request of Ziyād. Ziyād then sent a person to sit in the path of Abu Al-Aswad Al-Du'alī and instructed him to intentionally recite a portion of the Qur'ān incorrect. When Abu Al-Aswad Al-Du'alī passed by and heard him recite <u>incorrectly</u> the Qur'ān as follows:

أَنَّ ٱللَّهَ بَرِىٓءٌ مِّنَ ٱلْمُشْرِكِينَ وَرَسُولِهِ

'that Allāh is disassociated from the <u>disbelievers and his Messenger</u>' .

The correct recitation is:

أَنَّ ٱللَّهَ بَرِىٓءٌ مِّنَ ٱلْمُشْرِكِينَ وَرَسُولُهُ ۚ التَّوْبَةُ ٣

'that <u>Allāh and his Messenger</u> are disassociated from the disbelievers.'

Abu Al-Aswad Al-Du'alī became angry because he regarded this as a major mistake and exclaimed: *'Allāh is beyond disassociating his Messenger [from himself]'*. He then returned immediately to Ziyād and accepted the task of vowelising the Qur'ān.

Abu Al-Aswad Al-Du'alī requested thirty scholars from which he filtered and selected a scholar from the tribe of Abd al-Qays. Abu Al-Aswad Al-Du'alī requested him to mark the Muṣ-ḥaf with a different coloured ink as he recited the Qurān:

> *'If I open my lips, add a dot above the letter. If I make my lips round, add a dot to the side of the letter. If I lower my lip, place a dot under the letter. If I follow any of the vowels with a Ghunna, add two dots'.*

So the entire Muṣ-ḥaf was completed and this was the first step towards the vowelisation of the Qurān. The dots added by Abu Al-Aswad Al-Du'alī were called Naqt al-I'rāb and preceded the modern-day Fatḥa, Ḍamma, Kasra and Tashdīd.

Two students of Abu Al-Aswad Al-Du'alī; Naṣr bin 'Āsim Al-Laythī (died 90 AH) and Yahya bin Ya'mar (died before 90 AH) further developed the Arabic language by differentiating between similar letters using dots, which are called Naqt al-I'jām.

For example, the letter sheen (ش) was written without any dots like the letter seen (س) which became a challenge for bedouins and non-Arabs who embraced Islam and struggled to distinguish between the two letters.

Educated Arabs did not struggle for example reading the the word (شمس) (sun) without dots as this word was commonly used in their language, whereas non-Arabs could not have recognised this word as it was not used in their language.

This new system continued for about a century. However, this system also posed challenges of its own as it was easy to confuse the two groups of dots. Therefore, the dots of I'jām which indicate vowels were further developed by the linguist and grammarian Imām Al-Khalīl bin Ahmed Al-Farahīdī (died 170 AH).

Diacritical Vowels	Symbol
Imām Al-Khalīl developed the Fatḥah from a small angled Alif placed above the letter. The word Fatḥah itself means opening and refers to the opening of the sound of the letter. It represents a short /a/ sound like in the words 'cat' and 'sat'.	ـَ
For Ḍammah he placed a small Waw above the letter that represents a short /u/ sound like in the words 'shoe' and 'sue'. The word Ḍammah means to combine or bring close and refers to bringing close the lips in a circular shape.	ـُ
Kasrah originally was a small Yā below the letter that later developed into a small angled line taken from the head of the letter ي that represents the /i/ sound like in the words 'lip' and 'sip'. Kasrah means to break and refers to breaking the sound of the letter.	ـِ
For Tashdīd he used the little (w) symbol taken from the head of the letter ش without the dots, from the word شديد which means heavy.	ـّ
Lastly for a Sākin symbol he used the head of the letter ح without the dot, from the word خفيف which means light.	ـْ

Evolution of Arabic Alphabet -   Dots & Vowels

Evolution of Arabic *Dots & Vowels*	*Example*
Time of Revelation (13 BH)	سم الله الرحمں الرحم
Naqt al-I'rab - Abu Al-Aswad Al-Du'alī (16 BH - 69AH)	بسم اللّه الرّحمٮ الرّجيم
Naqt al I'jam - Naṣr bin 'Āsim (d. 89 AH) & Yahya bin Ya'mar (d. 100 AH)	بسم اللّه الرّحمٮ الرّجيم
Naqt al I'jam - Imam Al-Khalil bin Ahmed al-Farahīdī (110 AH - 170/175 AH)	بِسْمِ اللَّهِ الرَّحْمَٰنِ الرَّحِيمِ
Modern day with full Tashkeel and colour coded	بِسْمِ ٱللَّهِ ٱلرَّحْمَٰنِ ٱلرَّحِيمِ

Evolution of *Dots & Vowels*	*Example*
Time of Revelation (13 BH)	والسمس و صحها
Naqt al-I'rab - Abu Al-Aswad Al-Du'alī (16 BH - 69AH)	والتمبس و.صخها
Naqt al I'jam - Naṣr bin 'Āsim (d. 89 AH) & Yahya bin Ya'mar (d. 100 AH)	والثّمبس و.ضخها
Naqt al I'jam - Imam Al-Khalil bin Ahmed Al-Farahīdī (110 AH - 170/175 AH)	وَالشَّمْسِ وَضُحَاهَا
Modern day with full Tashkeel and colour coded	وَٱلشَّمْسِ وَضُحَاهَا

Anatomy of your mouth and throat

Front
bony hard palate
(roof of the mouth)

Teeth
Upper set

Lips
Upper & Lower

Teeth
Lower set

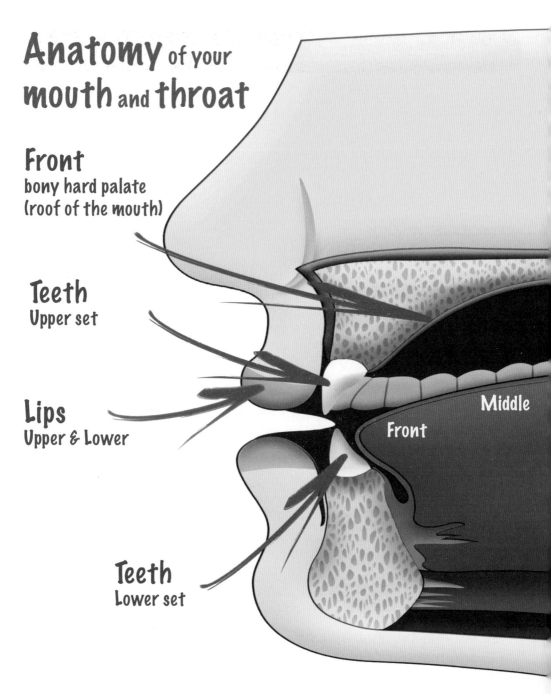

Middle

Front

Larygeal prominence of the
thyroid cartilage

So called..
Adams apple

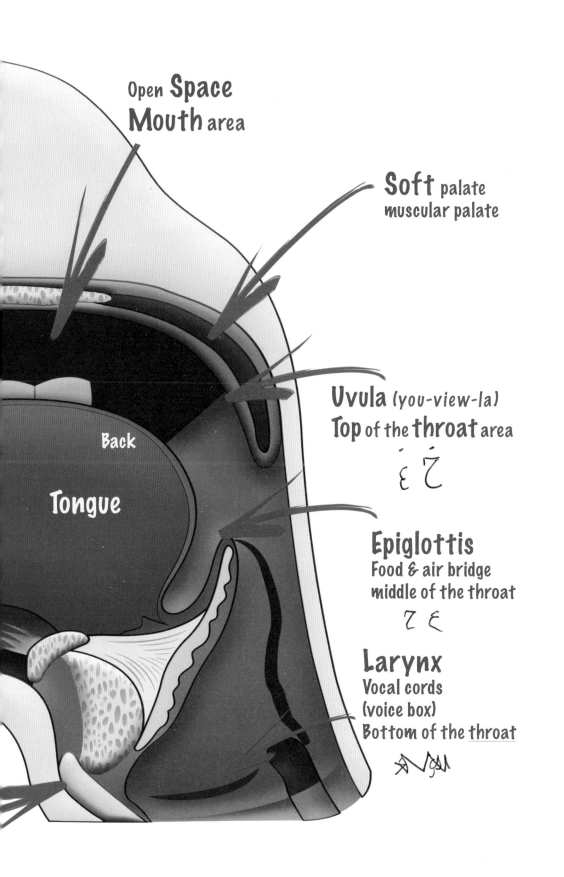

Open **Space**
Mouth area

Soft palate
muscular palate

Uvula (you-view-la)
Top of the **throat** area

ءُ ءۡ

Back

Tongue

Epiglottis
Food & air bridge
middle of the throat

ءۡ ءَ

Larynx
Vocal cords
(voice box)
Bottom of the <u>throat</u>

Incisors ●

are the **8** sharpe teeth (**4** upper and **4** lower) that we use to bite and cut food into small pieces.

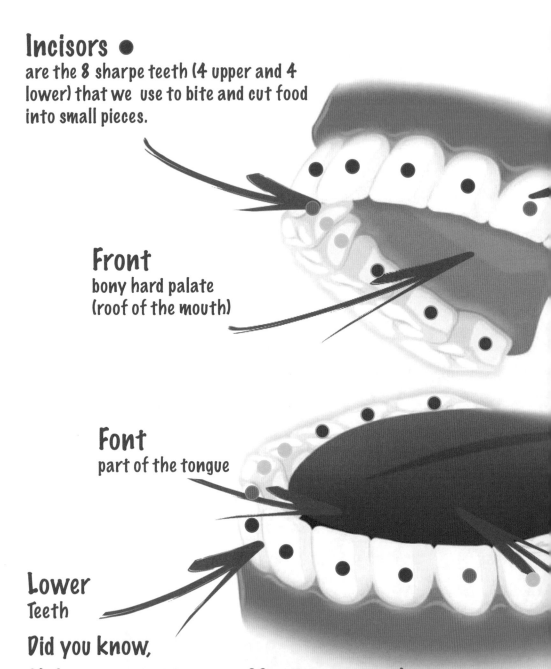

Front
bony hard palate
(roof of the mouth)

Font
part of the tongue

Lower
Teeth

Did you know,

Children and **babies** have **20 primary teeth** that begin to grow at **6 months** and be complete by the age of **3**. These **primary teeth** also known as **baby teeth** which are all pushed out by the age of **14** and replaced by **28** permanent adult teeth.

Anatomy of your Teeth and tongue

Canines ●
are the sharpe pointed teeth next to the incisors used to tear food. We all have 4 canines (2 upper and 2 lower). Children usually grow their first permanent canines between the ages of 9 and 12.

Premolars
are bigger than the incisors and canines used to grind food. Adults have 8 premolars (4 upper and 4 lower). Children usually grow their first permanent premolars between the ages of 10 and 12.

Molars ●
are the biggest teeth used to grind food. Adults have 12 molars (6 upper and 6 lower). Children only have 8 primary molars (4 upper and 4 lower).

Back
part of the tongue

Middle
part of the tongue

Transliteration Key

ء	'	ى	Y	ز	Z
ﻫ	H	ض	Ḍ	ذ	Dh
ع	'	ل	L	ث	Th
ح	Ḥ	ن	N	ظ	Ẓ
غ	Gh	ر	R	ب	B
خ	Kh	د	D	م	M
ق	Q	ت	T	و	W
ك	K	ط	Ṭ	ف	F
ش	Sh	س	S		
ج	J	ص	Ṣ		

Short Vowels		Long Vowels		Diphthongs	
ـَ	a	ـَا	ā	ـَو	aw
ـِ	i	ـِى	ī	ـَى	ay
ـُ	u	ـُو	ū		

SCAN ME

darulqurra.org

القاعدة السمنودية للمبتدئين

Chapter One
Introduction to Makhārij ul Ḥurūf

There are six letters that are recited from the throat called *Hurūf Al Ḥalqiyyah.*

Read all lessons without spelling and try to differentiate the sounds between each letter.

The first two letters are recited from the bottom part of the throat, located behind the 'so called' adams apple.

☞   Remember no letter can be recited from below this point (i.e. the chest).

الحروف
الحلقية

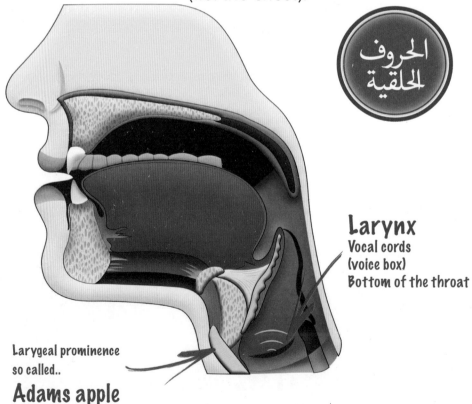

Larynx
Vocal cords
(voice box)
Bottom of the throat

Larygeal prominence
so called..
Adams apple

Practice

- Recite without spelling and try to differentiate the sound between each letter.
- Recite each letter short without an abrupt stop.
- Remember أ sound is much sharper and the ه sound.
- Each letter in this entire **chapter** should be repeated after the tutor making sure the learner differentiates between the two sounds.
  This can be achieved by a short pause between each letter.

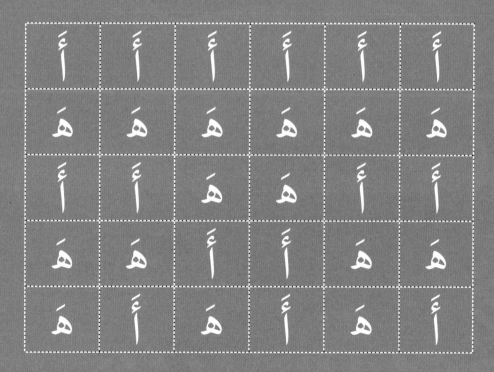

There are six letters that are recited from the throat called *Hurūf Al Ḥalqiyyah.*

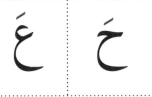

These two letters are recited from the middle part of the throat just above the Adam's apple.

☞ Remember to narrow the air passageway when reciting these two letters.

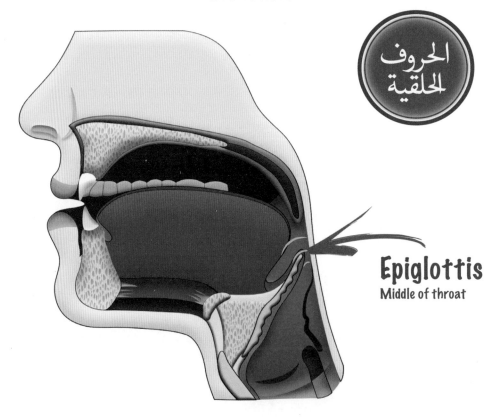

Epiglottis
Middle of throat

Practice

Remember (ع) sound is much sharper than the (ح) sound.

غَ	خَ	غَ	خَ	غَ	خَ
خَ	غَ	خَ	غَ	خَ	غَ
ةَ	خَ	أَ	خَ	غَ	خَ
خَ	ةَ	غَ	خَ	أَ	ةَ
خَ	أَ	غَ	أَ	ةَ	غَ
غَ	ةَ	خَ	غَ	أَ	غَ

There are six letters that are recited from the throat called *Hurūf Al Ḥalqiyyah*.

The last two letters are recited from the top part of the throat, just before the mouth area.

👉 Remember to raise the back of the tongue when reciting these two letters (creating a full mouth sound).

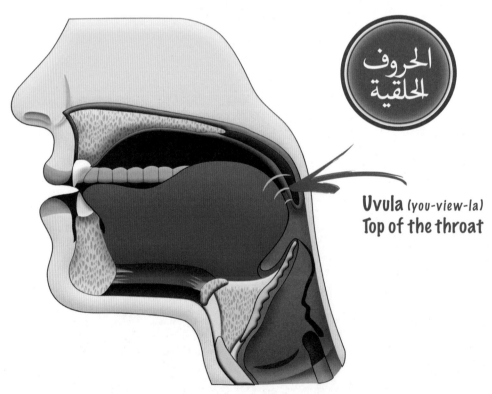

الحروف الحلقية

Uvula *(you-view-la)*
Top of the throat

Practice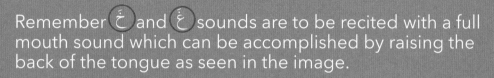

Remember ﺥ and ﻍ sounds are to be recited with a full mouth sound which can be accomplished by raising the back of the tongue as seen in the image.

خٌ	غٌ	خْ	غْ	خَ	غَ
غٍ	خٍ	خٌ	خْ	خٌ	خٌ
خْ	غَ	غْ	حَ	خْ	غٌ
هَ	غَ	خْ	هَ	أً	هَ
خَ	غْ	هْ	أً	غَ	حْ
حَ	هْ	أَ	غْ	خْ	حَ

Exercise

Match the letters to their correct Makhraj (articulation point).

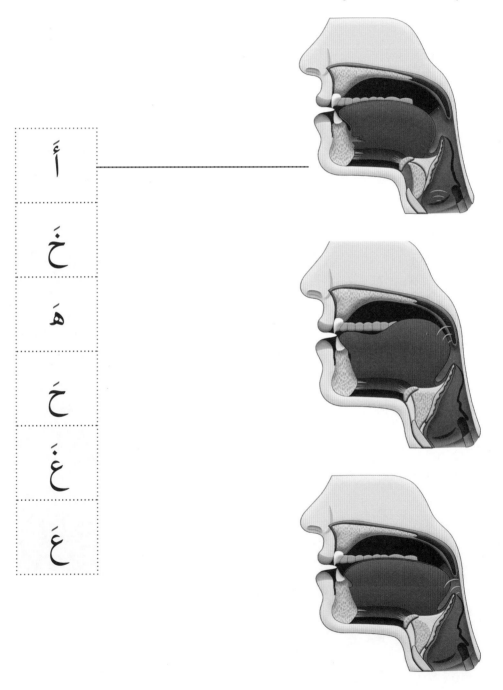

أَ	
خَ	
هَ	
حَ	
غَ	
عَ	

Revision 1.0 📖

Remember to continue reciting without spelling and to differentiate the sounds between each letter clearly.

أَ	هَ	غَ	خَ	أَ	هَ
خَ	غَ	أَ	غَ	خَ	أَ
حَ	خَ	أَ	هَ	غَ	هَ
هَ	أَ	حَ	خَ	هَ	حَ
غَ	هَ	خَ	غَ	أَ	حَ
غَ	أَ	حَ	حَ	هَ	غَ
حَ	غَ	حَ	غَ	أَ	هَ
غَ	أَ	غَ	غَ	أَ	حَ
غَ	أَ	خَ	خَ	أَ	غَ
غَ	هَ	حَ	خَ	أَ	غَ

There are two letters that are recited from the back of the tongue called *Hurūf Al Lahwiyyah.*

قَ   كَ

These two letters are recited from the back of the tongue, closest to the throat.

حروف
اللهوية

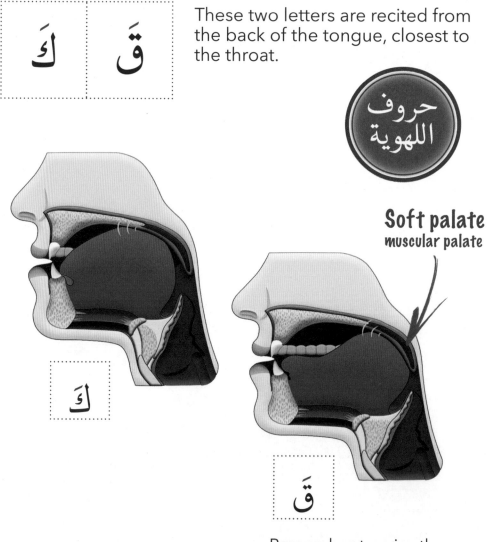

Soft palate
muscular palate

كَ

قَ

Remember to raise the back of the tongue ⇧

Practice 📖

Remember must be recited with a full mouth sound by raising the back of the tongue and ﻛَ should be recited with a light empty mouth sound by keeping the back of the tongue low.

قَ	كَ	كَ	قَ	قَ	كَ
كَ	قَ	قَ	كَ	كَ	قَ
قَ	كَ	قَ	كَ	كَ	قَ
قَ	كَ	كَ	قَ	كَ	قَ
قَ	كَ	قَ	كَ	قَ	كَ
كَ	قَ	كَ	كَ	قَ	قَ

Exercise

Match the letters to their correct Makhraj (articulation point).

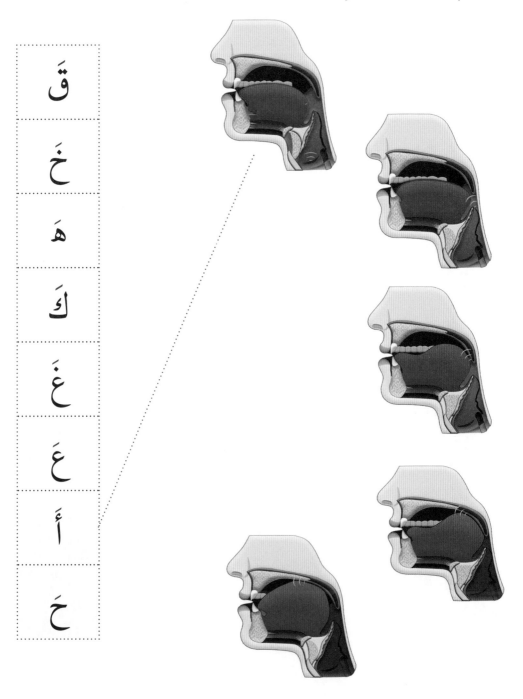

قَ

خَ

هَ

كَ

غَ

عَ

أَ

حَ

Revision 1.1

Remember to continue reciting without spelling and to differentiate the sounds between each letter clearly.

أَ	قَ	غَ	خَ	قَ	كَ
نْخَ	غْ	قَ	هْ	نْخَ	كَ
حَ	نْخَ	كَ	قَ	غْ	هَ
قَ	أَ	هَ	نْخَ	كَ	حَ
قَغْ	كَ	قَ	عَ	هْ	حَ
قَعْ	عَ	حَ	غْ	أَ	كَ
هَغْ	قَ	حَ	عَ	قَ	نْخَ
عَ	قَ	عَ	قَ	أَ	حَ
عَ	كَ	قَ	حَ	هَ	نْغ
قَ	أَ	كَ	نْخَ	قَ	نْغ

There are four letters that are recited from the mid-section of the tongue called *Hurūf Ash-Shajariyyah.*

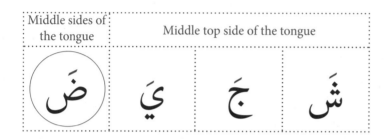

Middle sides of the tongue	Middle top side of the tongue		
ضَ	يَ	جَ	شَ

Letter ﺽ will be discussed in the next lesson.

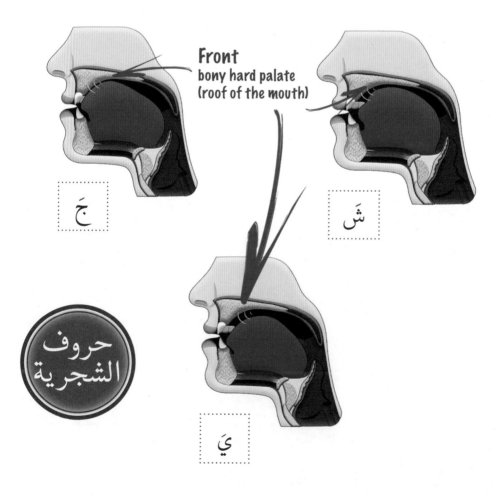

Front
bony hard palate
(roof of the mouth)

جَ

شَ

حروف الشجرية

يَ

Practice

Remember all three letters should be recited with a light empty mouth sound by keeping the back of the tongue low.

يَ	جَ	شَ	يَ	جَ	ش
جَ	شَ	يَ	جَ	شَ	يَ
شَ	يَ	جَ	شَ	جَ	يَ
جَ	يَ	شَ	يَ	شَ	جَ
شَ	يَ	جَ	شَ	جَ	يَ
شَ	جَ	يَ	جَ	شَ	يَ

Exercise

Match the letters to their correct Makhraj (articulation point).

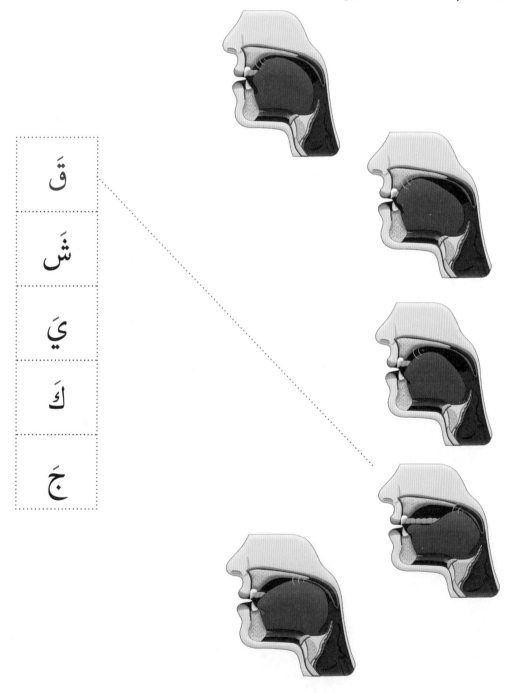

قَ

شَ

يَ

كَ

جَ

Revision 1.2 📖

Remember to continue reciting without spelling and to differentiate the sound between each letter clearly.

يَ	شَ	غَ	جَ	قَ	شَ
شَ	غَ	قَ	يَ	خَ	كَ
يَ	خَ	جَ	قَ	غَ	شَ
قَ	أَ	هَ	يَ	جَ	حَ
غَ	شَ	جَ	عَ	شَ	حَ
يَ	أَ	شَ	حَ	قَ	غَ
قَ	كَ	حَ	غَ	يَ	كَ
هَ	قَ	حَ	عَ	جَ	خَ
غَ	يَ	عَ	قَ	أَ	حَ
عَ	أَ	جَ	حَ	هَ	يَ

There is only one unique letter that is recited from the sides (middle) of the tongue which has been categorised by Imām Ibrahīm Alī Shehāta Al-Samanūdi as the final letter of *Hurūf Ash-Shajariyyah*.

The early Arabic grammarians and scholars described Arabic as the language of (ضاد) as this letter has a sound, unique to the Arabic language.

This letter is recited from either side (middle) of the tongue.

☞   Remember to trap the sound using the upper molars and premolars whilst raising the back of the tongue when reciting this letter.

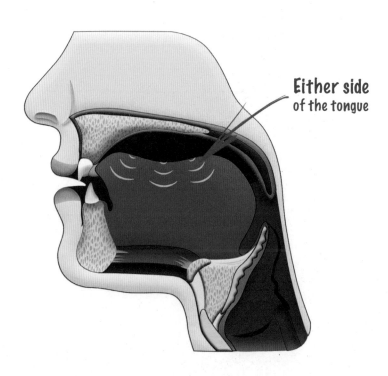

Either side of the tongue

Practice

Remember to recite this letter with a full mouth sound by raising the back of the tongue.

ضَ	ضَ	ضَ	ضَ	ضَ	ضَ
جَ	شَ	ضَ	جَ	شَ	يَ
شَ	ضَ	جَ	شَ	ضَ	يَ
ضَ	يَ	ضَ	ضَ	جَ	ضَ
شَ	ضَ	جَ	شَ	ضَ	يَ
ضَ	جَ	يَ	جَ	ضَ	يَ

Exercise

Match the letters to their correct Makhraj (articulation point).

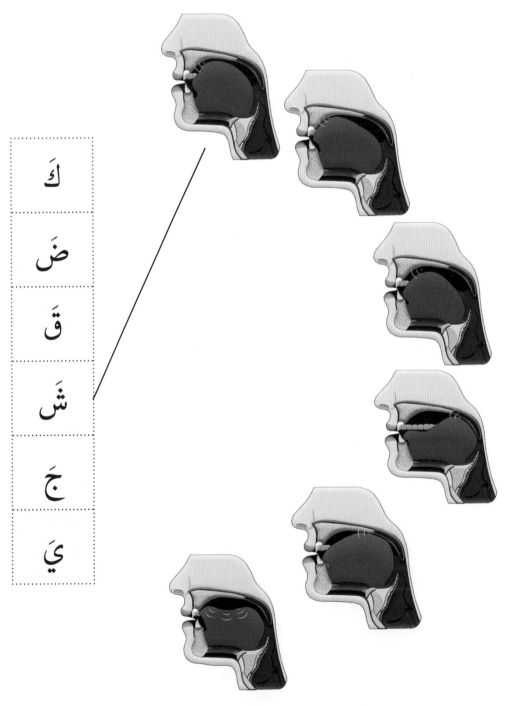

كَ

ضَ

قَ

شَ

جَ

يَ

Revision 1.3 📖

Remember to continue reciting without spelling and to
differentiate the sounds between each letter clearly.

ضَ	شَ	غَ	ضَ	قَ	شَ
شَ	غَ	قَ	يَ	ضَ	كَ
يَ	خَ	ضَ	قَ	غَ	شَ
ضَ	أَ	هَ	يَ	جَ	ضَ
غَ	شَ	جَ	عَ	شَ	حَ
ضَ	أَ	شَ	حَ	قَ	غَ
ضَ	كَ	حَ	غَ	يَ	كَ
هَ	قَ	حَ	عَ	جَ	خَ
غَ	يَ	عَ	ضَ	أَ	حَ
عَ	أَ	جَ	حَ	هَ	ضَ

There are three letters recited from the front part of the tongue but not from a single place called Hurūf Dhalqiyyah.

رَ   نَ   لَ

When reciting نَ the sound will split between the mouth and the noise.

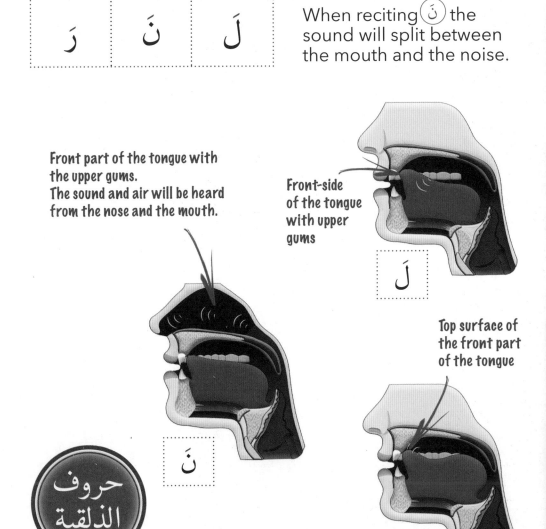

Front part of the tongue with the upper gums.
The sound and air will be heard from the nose and the mouth.

Front-side of the tongue with upper gums

لَ

Top surface of the front part of the tongue

نَ

حروف الذلقية

رَ

Practice

Remember to recite the ﺭ with a full mouth sound and a little roll of the tip of the tongue.

رَ	نَ	لَ	رَ	نَ	لَ
نَ	لَ	رَ	رَ	لَ	نَ
لَ	رَ	نَ	لَ	رَ	رَ
رَ	نَ	لَ	لَ	رَ	نَ
رَ	لَ	نَ	نَ	رَ	لَ
لَ	نَ	رَ	نَ	لَ	رَ

Exercise

Match the letters to their correct Makhraj (articulation point).

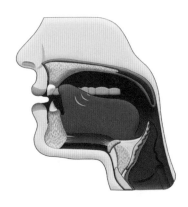

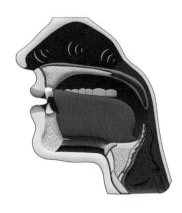

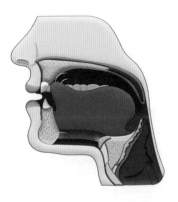

Revision 1.4 📖

Remember to continue reciting without spelling and to differentiate the sound between each letter clearly.

خَ	غَ	عَ	حَ	هَ	أَ
ضَ	يَ	جَ	شَ	كَ	قَ
حَ	هَ	أَ	رَ	نَ	لَ
شَ	كَ	قَ	خَ	غَ	عَ
رَ	نَ	لَ	ضَ	يَ	جَ
غَ	قَ	حَ	رَ	أَ	ضَ
لَ	كَ	رَ	حَ	نَ	ضَ
خَ	جَ	عَ	رَ	قَ	هَ
رَ	نَ	ضَ	عَ	نَ	نَ
ضَ	هَ	نَ	رَ	لَ	كَ

There are three letters that are recited from the front of the tongue called *Hurūf An-Niṭa'iyyah*.

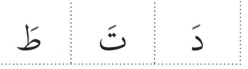

These three letters are recited from the front part of the tongue along with the upper incisors.

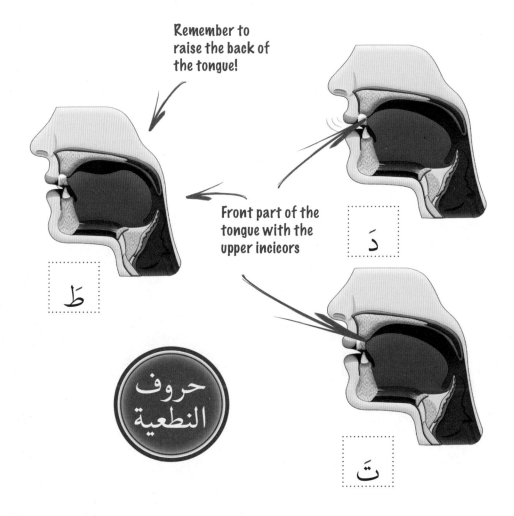

Remember to raise the back of the tongue!

Front part of the tongue with the upper incicors

حروف النطعية

Practice

Remember to recite the ظ with a full mouth sound by raising the back of the tongue.

طْ	تَ	دَ	طْ	تَ	دَ
تَ	دَ	طْ	تَ	دَ	طْ
دَ	طْ	تَ	دَ	طْ	تَ
طْ	تَ	طْ	دَ	تَ	دَ
دَ	تَ	طْ	دَ	طْ	تَ
طْ	دَ	تَ	دَ	طْ	دَ

Exercise

Match the letters to their correct Makhraj (articulation point).

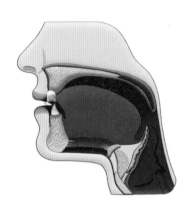

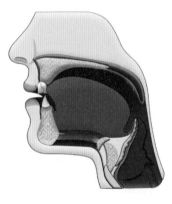

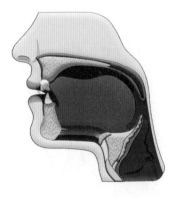

Revision 1.5

Remember to continue reciting without spelling and differentiating the sounds between each letter clearly.

خَ	غَ	عَ	حَ	هَ	أَ
ضَ	يَ	جَ	شَ	كَ	قَ
دَ	طَ	تَ	رَ	نَ	لَ
شَ	طَ	قَ	تَ	طَ	ثَ
ثَ	طَ	دَ	ضَ	تَ	جَ
ثَ	قَ	طَ	رَ	أَ	ضَ
لَ	كَ	رَ	دَ	طَ	حَ
غَ	جَ	نَ	طَ	قَ	هَ
رَ	خَ	ضَ	عَ	ضَ	نَ
ضَ	طَ	نَ	ثَ	لَ	طَ

There are three letters that are recited from the front of the tongue called *Hurūf Al Asliyyah.*

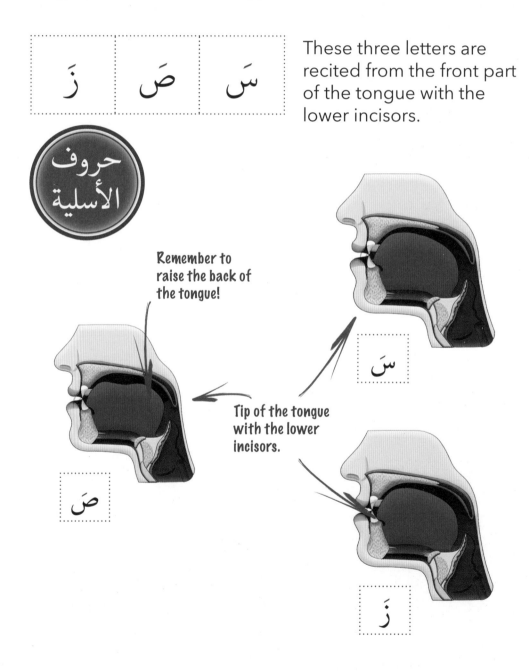

These three letters are recited from the front part of the tongue with the lower incisors.

سَ   صَ ص   زَ ز

حروف الأسلية

Remember to raise the back of the tongue!

Tip of the tongue with the lower incisors.

سَ

صَ

زَ

Practice

Remember to recite the ﺽ with a full mouth sound by raising the back of the tongue.

سَ	صَ	زَ	سَ	صَ	زَ
زَ	سَ	صَ	زَ	سَ	صَ
صَ	زَ	سَ	صَ	زَ	سَ
سَ	صَ	زَ	صَ	سَ	زَ
سَ	زَ	صَ	زَ	صَ	سَ
صَ	زَ	سَ	صَ	زَ	سَ
صَ	زَ	صَ	زَ	سَ	صَ
صَ	زَ	سَ	صَ	سَ	زَ

Exercise

Match the letters to their correct Makhraj (articulation point).

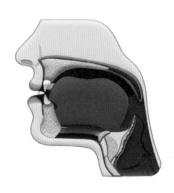

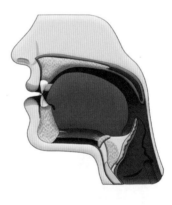

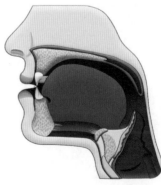

Revision 1.6 📖

Remember to continue reciting without spelling and differentiating the sounds between each letter clearly.

خَ	غَ	عَ	حَ	هَ	أَ
ضَ	يَ	جَ	شَ	كَ	قَ
دَ	طَ	تَ	رَ	نَ	لَ
زَ	سَ	قَ	زَ	صَ	سَ
صَ	زَ	دَ	ضَ	سَ	صَ
قَ	خَ	غَ	زَ	طَ	ضَ
حَ	هَ	أَ	صَ	سَ	يَ
رَ	زَ	ضَ	دَ	طَ	صَ
ضَ	طَ	خَ	صَ	جَ	زَ
صَ	زَ	رَ	زَ	قَ	ضَ

There are three letters that are recited from the front part of the tongue called *Hurūf Al Lithawiyyah.*

These three letters are recited from the front part of the tongue with the edge of the upper incisors.

Remember to raise the back of the tongue!

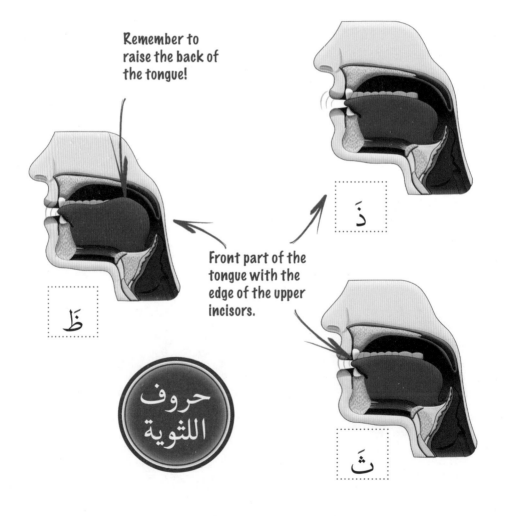

Front part of the tongue with the edge of the upper incisors.

حروف اللثوية

Practice

Remember to recite the ﻆ with a full mouth sound by raising the back of the tongue.

ظَ	ثَ	ذَ	ظَ	ثَ	ذَ
ثَ	ذَ	ظَ	ثَ	ذَ	ظَ
ذَ	ظَ	ثَ	ذَ	ظَ	ثَ
ظَ	ذَ	ظَ	ظَ	ثَ	ظَ
ذَ	ثَ	ظَ	ثَ	ظَ	ذَ
ظَ	ذَ	ثَ	ذَ	ظَ	ثَ

Exercise

Match the letters to their correct Makhraj (articulation point).

ظَ

ثَ

ذَ

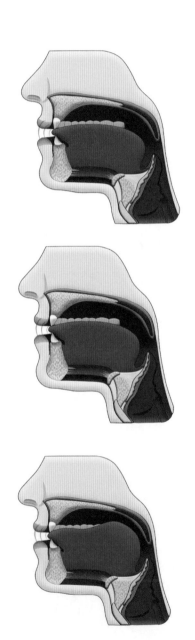

Revision 1.7 📖

Remember to continue reciting without spelling and differentiating the sound between each letter clearly.

خَ	غَ	عَ	حَ	هَ	أَ
ضَ	يَ	جَ	شَ	كَ	قَ
دَ	طَ	تَ	رَ	نَ	لَ
ذَ	ثَ	ظَ	زَ	صَ	سَ
ظَ	طَ	ذَ	دَ	ضَ	صَ
قَ	خَ	غَ	ظَ	طَ	ضَ
حَ	هَ	أَ	ثَ	سَ	يَ
ثَ	طَ	ذَ	دَ	طَ	تَ
ضَ	ظَ	خَ	حَ	جَ	ثَ
ظَ	طَ	زَ	رَ	ظَ	ذَ

There are four letters that are recited from the lips that are called *Hurūf Ash-Shafawiyyah.*

حروف الشفوية

وَ	بَ	مَ	فَ

Outer dry part of lips

مَ

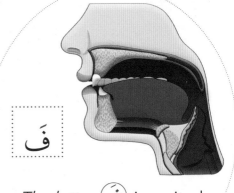

فَ

The letter (فَ) is recited using *the lower lip only.*

وَ

بَ

Inner wet part of lips

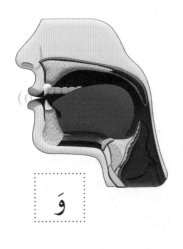

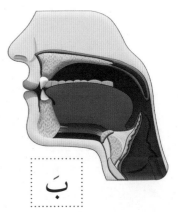

Letters مَ بَ وَ are recited by using *both of the lips.*

Practice

Remember to recite all four letters with an empty mouth sound by lowering the back of the tongue.

فَ	مَ	بَ	وَ	فَ	مَ
وَ	بَ	فَ	مَ	مَ	بَ
فَ	وَ	مَ	فَ	بَ	وَ
بَ	فَ	وَ	مَ	بَ	وَ
مَ	بَ	وَ	فَ	فَ	مَ
فَ	وَ	بَ	وَ	مَ	فَ

Exercise

Match the letters to their correct Makhraj (articulation point).

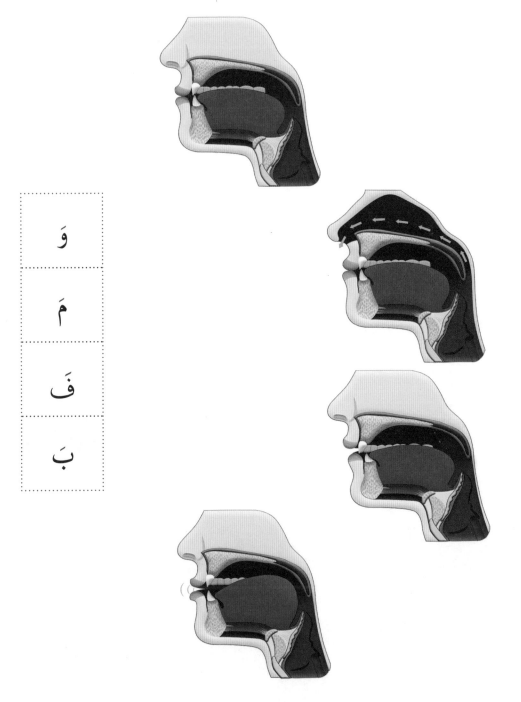

وَ

مَ

فَ

بَ

Revision 1.8 📖

Remember to continue reciting without spelling and differentiating the sound between each letter clearly.

خَ	غَ	عَ	حَ	هَ	أَ
ضَ	يَ	جَ	شَ	كَ	قَ
دَ	طَ	ثَ	رَ	نَ	لَ
ذَ	ثَ	ظَ	زَ	صَ	سَ
ظَ	طَ	وَ	بَ	مَ	فَ
ظَ	طَ	زَ	مَ	فَ	ضَ
قَ	فَ	مَ	ظَ	بَ	ثَ
وَ	مَ	أَ	ثَ	سَ	يَ
رَ	فَ	ثَ	بَ	فَ	مَ
ضَ	ظَ	وَ	بَ	جَ	وَ

Summary - Makhārij ul Hurūf

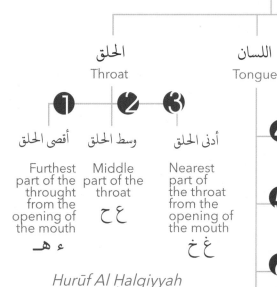

الحلق
Throat

اللسان
Tongue

① أقصى الحلق

Furthest part of the throught from the opening of the mouth

ء هـ

Hurūf Al Ḥalqiyyah

② وسط الحلق

Middle part of the throat

ع ح

③ أدنى الحلق

Nearest part of the throat from the opening of the mouth

غ خ

④ أقصى اللسان   ق

Furthest part of the tongue

⑤ أقصى اللسان   ك

Furthest part of the tongue towards the opening of the mouth

⑥ وسط اللسان   ش ج ى

Middle part of the tongue with help of the hard palate

⑦ حافة اللسان   ض

Either (middle) sides of the tongue with the help of Al Aḍrās teeth.

⑧ أدنى حافة اللسان   ل

Recited from the front part of the tongue with the gums of your upper incisors.

⑨ طرف اللسان   ن

Front part of the tongue with the gums of your upper front two incisors.

⑩ طرف اللسان   ر

Top surface of the front part of the tongue with the gums of your upper incisors

⑪ طرف اللسان   د ت ط

Front of the tongue with the roots of upper incisors.

⑫ رأس اللسان   س ز ص

Tip of the tongue with the lower incisors.

⑬ طرف اللسان   ذ ث ظ

Front part of the tongue with the edge of the upper incisors.

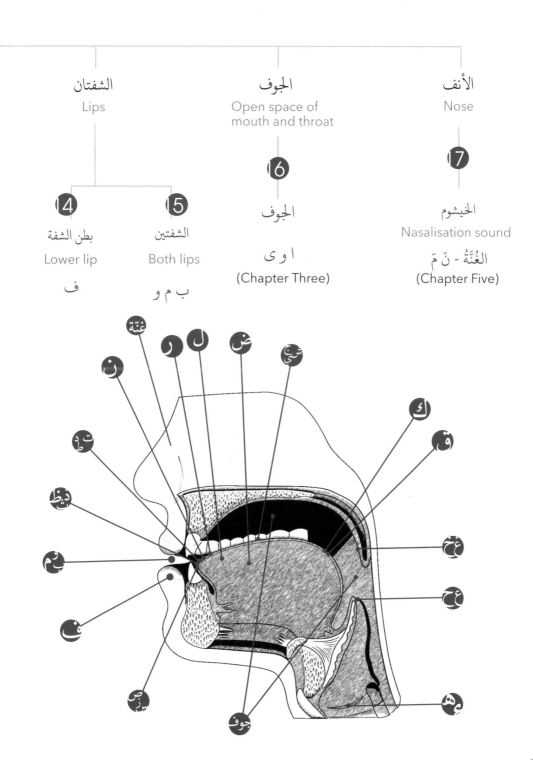

الشفتان
Lips

الجوف
Open space of
mouth and throat

الأنف
Nose

بطن الشفة
Lower lip
ف

الشفتين
Both lips
ب م و

الجوف
ا و ى
(Chapter Three)

الخيشوم
Nasalisation sound
الغُنَّةُ - نّ مّ
(Chapter Five)

45

There are seven letters permanently recited with a full mouth sound (Code: خُصَّ ضَغْطٍ قِظ) by raising the back of the tongue.

ظَ ‖ صَ ‖ خَ

قَ ‖ غَ ‖ ضَ

طَ

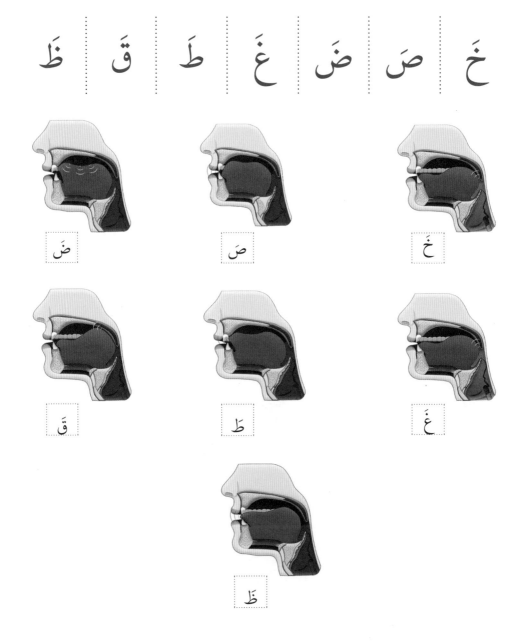

Practice

- Recite without spelling and try to differentiate the sound between each letter.

- Recite each letter short without an abrupt stop.

- Remember to recite all the letters with a full mouth sound by raising the back of the tongue.

خَ	ضَ	ظَ	قَ	طَ	غَ
صَ	ضَ	ضَ	طَ	ظَ	قَ	خَ
ضَ	غَ	خَ	صَ	طَ	ظَ
قَ	ضَ	صَ	ضَ	غَ	خَ
صَ	ضَ	خَ	غَ	طَ	ظَ
ضَ	طَ	ظَ	قَ	غَ	خَ

Exercise
Word Search

H	A	L	Q	E	R	W	AN	Q	L
U	AL	L	J	N	V	B	S	S	I
R	A	Q	E	AN	F	G	H	J	T
Ū	F	U	L	L	M	O	U	T	H
F	AL	L	A	H	W	I	Y	Y	A
M	A	K	H	R	A	J	O	Z	W
J	B	O	P	M	B	V	F	H	I
AN	N	I	T	A	I	Y	Y	A	Y
D	D	N	N	AL	A	AN	AN	W	Y
S	H	A	F	A	W	I	Y	Y	A

- Makhraj
- Hurūf
- Halq
- Full Mouth
- Shafawiyyah
- Lithawiyyah
- *An-Niṭaʻiyyah*
- *Al Lahwiyyah*

Revision 1.9 📖

Remember to continue reciting without spelling and to identify the full mouth letters.

خَ	غَ	عَ	ضَ	نَ	أَ
ضَ	يَ	جَ	شَ	كَ	قَ
طَ	تَ	قَ	رَ	ضَ	لَ
ظَ	ثَ	ذَ	ضَ	صَ	سَ
ظَ	طَ	وَ	قَ	مَ	خَ
قَ	فَ	مَ	ظَ	قَ	ضَ
وَ	مَ	أَ	ثَ	سَ	يَ
رَ	بَ	ضَ	دَ	فَ	مَ
ضَ	ظَ	صَ	حَ	جَ	وَ
ظَ	صَ	قَ	مَ	خَ	ضَ

Letters of the Arabic alphabet presented according to their shapes. Concentrate on the shapes of letters, rather than memorising the sequence.

- Identify similarities between the letters.

- Continue without spelling and try to differentiate the sound between each letter.

- Recite each letter short without an abrupt stop.

- Remember to continue differentiating between full mouth and empty mouth sounds.

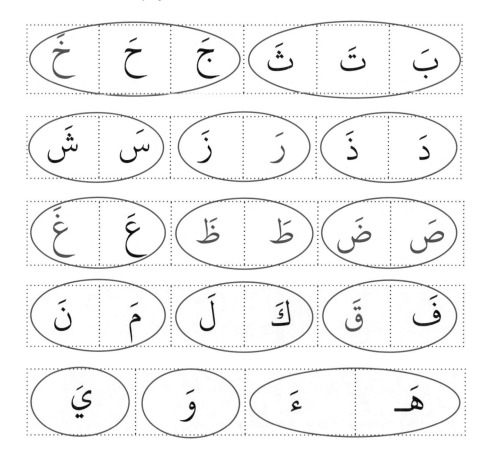

Exercise
Word Search

R	E	S	P	E	C	T	Y	T
H	Q	U	R	A	N	Y	H	E
T	A	K	Q	G	D	Q	Y	A
U	I	A	L	C	P	L	I	C
O	D	Z	A	V	I	O	A	H
M	A	S	J	I	D	J	T	E
H	A	P	P	I	N	E	T	R
L	I	S	U	N	N	A	H	Y
H	A	P	P	I	N	E	S	S
J	A	N	N	A	H	C	A	J

- Masjid
- Teacher
- Quran
- Qaida
- Jannah
- Sunnah
- *Respect*
- *Happiness*

In this lesson, concentrate on the shapes of letters and identify similarities between them.

 Remember the dots will always remain the same.

- Continue without spelling and try to differentiate the sounds between each letter.
- Recite each letter short without an abrupt stop.
- Remember to continue differentiating between the full mouth and empty mouth sounds.

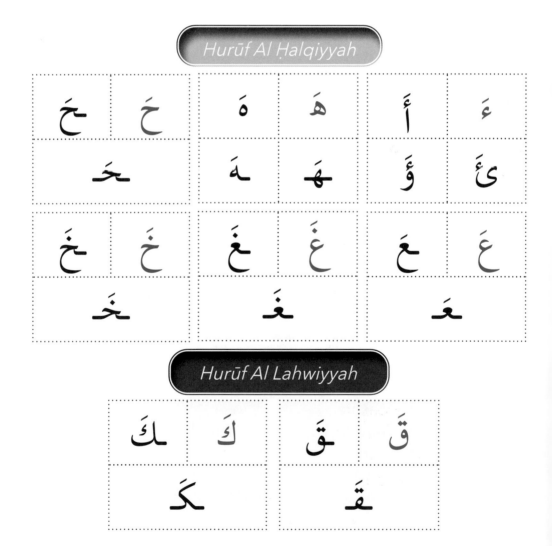

Hurūf Al Ḥalqiyyah

Hurūf Al Lahwiyyah

Hurūf Al Shajarriyyah

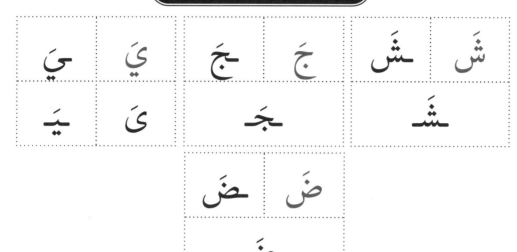

يَ	يَ	جَ	جَ	شَ	شَ
يَ	ىَ		جَ		شَ
		ضَ	ضَ		
			ضَ		

Hurūf Dhalqiyyah

رَ	رَ	نَ	نَ	لَ	لَ
	رَ		نَ		لَ

Hurūf An-Niṭa'iyyah

طَ	طَ	ةَ	تَ	دَ	دَ
	طَ	ةَ	تَ		دَ

53

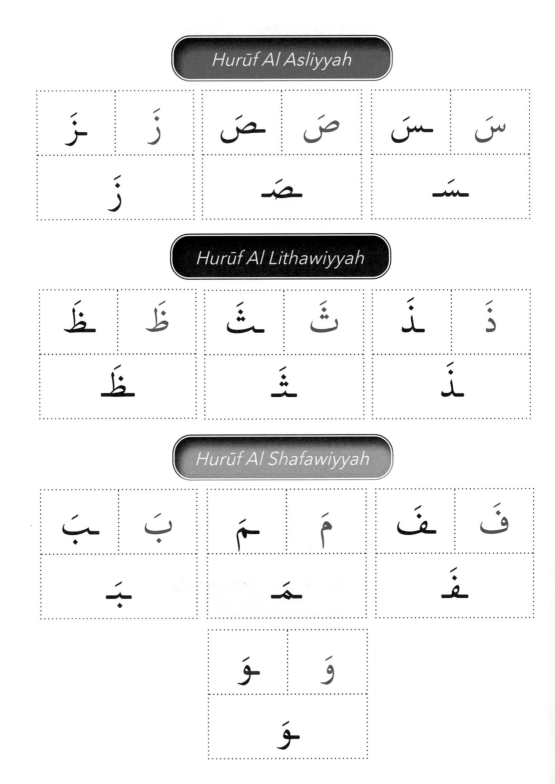

Exercise

Connect the matching letters.

وَ	ـزَ	كَ	نَـ
زَ	ـسَـ	لَ	ـغَـ
طَ	ـتَـ	أَ	ـهَـ
ظَ	ـطَ	نَ	ـضَـ
فَ	ـظَـ	غَ	ـشَـ
تَ	ـصَـ	هَ	ـخَـ
سَ	ـوَ	خَ	ـكَـ
صَ	ـبَـ	شَ	ـلَـ
مَ	ـفَـ	قَ	ؤَ
بَ	ـمَـ	ضَ	ـقَـ

In this lesson, concentrate on the shapes of letters and identify the similarities between them whilst connecting with other letters to form short words.

- Continue without spelling and try to differentiate the sound between each letter.

- Recite each letter short without an abrupt stop.

- Remember continue to differentiate between full mouth and empty mouth sounds.

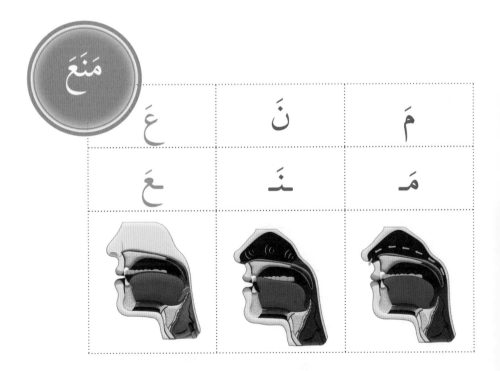

عَ	نَ	مَ
عَ	نَ	مَ

مَنَعَ

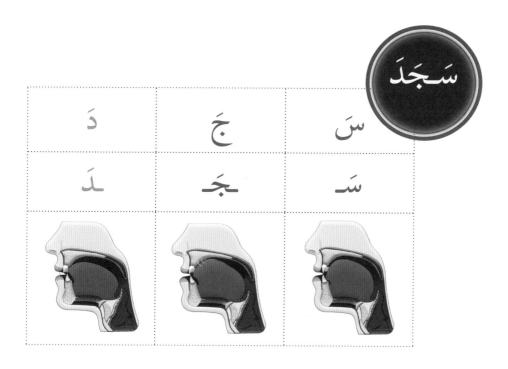

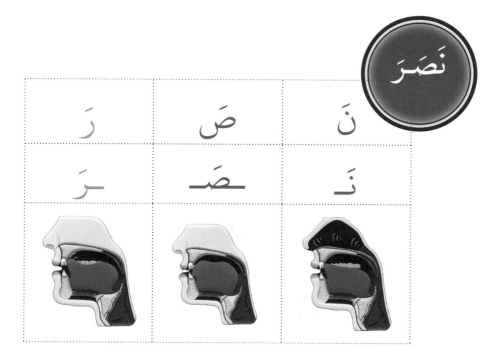

57

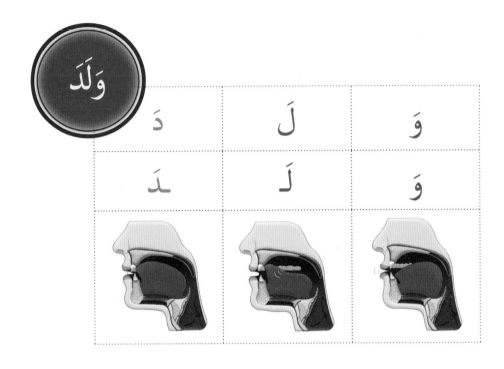

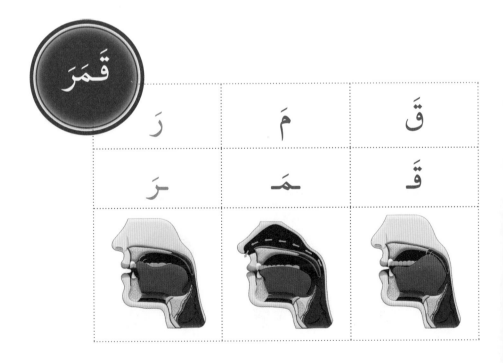

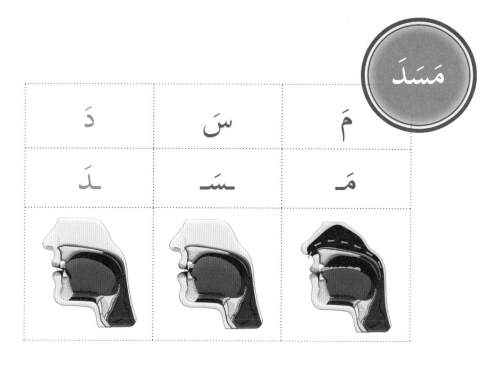

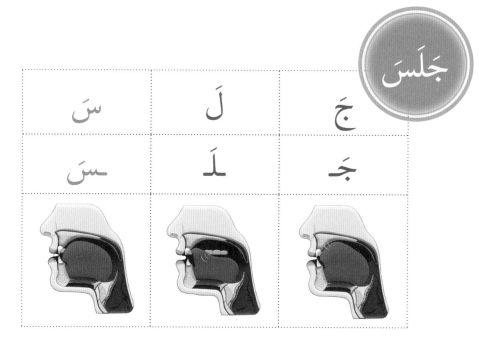

59

In this lesson, continue concentrating on the shapes of letters and identify the similarities between them whilst connecting with other letters to form short words.

- Continue without spelling and try to differentiate the sound between each letter.
- Recite each letter short without an abrupt stop.
- Remember continue to differentiate between the full mouth and empty mouth sounds.

حَضَرَ	رَ	ضَ	خَ	مَسَحَ	حَ	سَ	مَ
	رَ	ـضَـ	حَـ		ـحَ	ـسَـ	مَـ
رَزَقَ	قَ	زَ	رَ	أَمَنَ	نَ	مَ	أ
	قَ	زَ	رَ		ـنَ	ـمَـ	أ
غَسَلَ	لَ	سَ	غَ	دَفَنَ	نَ	فَ	دَ
	لَ	سَـ	غَـ		ـنَ	ـفَ	دَ
حَرَثَ	ثَ	رَ	خَ	وَصَلَ	لَ	صَ	وَ
	ثَ	ـرَ	حَـ		ـلَ	ـصَـ	وَ
قَرَضَ	ضَ	رَ	قَ	أَكَلَ	لَ	كَ	أ
	ضَ	ـرَ	قَ		ـلَ	ـكَـ	أ

زَحَف	ف حَ زَ	ظَهَرَ	رَ	هَ	ظ	
	فَ حَ زَ		ـرَ	هـ	ظـ	
عَبَسَ	س بَ عَ	سَكَبَ	بَ	كَ	سَ	
	سَ بَـ عَـ		بَ	كَـ	سَـ	
بَصَمَ	مَ صَ بَ	صَدَقَ	قَ	دَ	صَ	
	مَـ صَـ بَـ		قَ	دَ	صَـ	
لَحَظَ	ظَ حَ لَ	ظَلَمَ	مَ	لَ	ظ	
	ظَـ حَـ لَـ		مَـ	لَـ	ظـ	
نَظَرَ	رَ ظَ نَ	طَلَعَ	عَ	لَ	طَ	
	ـرَ ظَـ نَـ		عَ	لَـ	طَـ	
غَضَبَ	بَ ضَ غَ	خَطَبَ	بَ	طَ	خَ	
	بَـ ضَـ غَـ		بَ	طَـ	خَـ	
رَفَعَ	عَ فَ رَ	بَصَمَ	مَ	صَ	بَ	
	عَـ فَـ رَ		مَـ صَـ	صَـ	بَـ	

In this lesson, concentrate on the entire word.

- Continue without spelling and try to differentiate the sound between each letter.
- Recite each letter short without an abrupt stop.
- Remember to continue differentiating between full mouth and empty mouth sounds.

| كَتَبَ | بَ ت كَ | بَطَشَ | شَ طَ بَ |
| | بَ ـتَ كَ | | شَ طَ بَـ |

| جَلَسَ | سَ لَ جَ | نَصَرَ | نَ صَ رَ |
| | سَ ـلَ جَـ | | نَـ ـصَـ رَ |

| قَرَأَ | أَ رَ قَ | أَخَذَ | أَ خَ ذَ |
| | أَ ـرَ قَـ | | أَ خَـ ـذَ |

| سَأَلَ | لَ أَ سَ | أَمَرَ | أَ مَ رَ |
| | لَ ـأَ سَـ | | أَ مَـ رَ |

عَرَضَ	نَهَرَ	خَطَبَ	نَصَفَ	سَمَعَ
نَبَضَ	قَنَصَ	مَسَحَ	حَسَدَ	خَلَدَ
فَطَرَ	فَتَنَ	غَمَرَ	صَهَرَ	نَصَفَ
لَمَسَ	شَمَعَ	وَعَظَ	خَلَقَ	أَثَرَ
رَقَدَ	طَرَقَ	أَكَلَ	شَفَعَ	تَرَكَ
هَمَزَ	أَحَدَ	سَأَلَ	مَلَكَ	رَكَضَ
وَرَدَ	وَلَدَ	غَضَبَ	هَمَسَ	جَثَمَ
بَسَطَ	هَتَفَ	كَتَبَ	نَقَصَ	نَكَصَ
فَصَدَقَ	حَلَفَ	فَوَهَبَ	بَسَطَ	فَشَكَرَ
وَبَسَرَ	عَبَسَ	فَوَقَعَ	قَفَزَ	فَنَبَتَ
فَعَجَنَ	وَنَخَلَ	طَحَنَ	فَتَحَ	وَعَدَلَ
وَجَلَسَ	دَخَلَ	وَسَجَدَ	رَكَعَ	فَعَرَفَ
فَشَرَحَ	غَفَرَ	ضَجَعَ	هَضَمَ	صَنَعَ
فَحَشَرَ	فَسَأَلَ	فَسَئِلَ	غَلَبَ	مَنَعَ
سَعَدَ	فَنَجَحَ	وَكَتَبَ	قَرَأَ	فَنَظَرَ
خَلَقَ	جَزَمَ	نَصَرَ	فَتَحَ	عَبَسَ

Exercise
Word Search

لَ	خَ	دَ	قَ	رَ	صَ	دَ	قَ	رَ
مَ	خَ	دَ	صَ	فَ	لَ	ا	صَ	فَ
رَ	عَ	قَ	وَ	تَ	حَ	تَ	دَ	رَ
ضَ	قَ	رَ	ا	شَ	ا	خَ	دَ	حَ
ا	صَ	فَ	رَ	بَ	لَ	غَ	خَ	دَ
دَ	لَ	بَ	ا	خَ	دَ	حَ	تَ	فَ
قَ	رَ	فَ	مَ	زَ	جَ	مَ	قَ	رَ
صَ	فَ	فَ	غَ	خَ	خَ	دَ	صَ	فَ

مَرَضَ	رَقَدَ
قَصَدَ	فَتَحَ
وَقَعَ	جَزَمَ
صَلَحَ	بَلَدَ
غَلَبَ	حَشَرَ
فَرَحَ	دَخَلَ

Exercise
Word Search

صَ	لَ	أ	سَ	صَ	سَ	مَ	ضَ	هَ
حَ	أ	جَ	دَ	حَ	صَ	قَ	حَ	أ
كَ	صَ	بَ	بَ	دَ	قَ	دَ	فَ	صَ
عَ	صَ	رَ	دَ	حَ	أ	دَ	ا	غَ
بَ	أ	ضَ	كَ	كَ	صَ	ا	فَ	عَ
سَ	حَ	أ	لَ	دَ	كَ	رَ	قَ	قَ
صَ	كَ	صَ	قَ	حَ	أ	ضَ	كَ	رَ
عَ	مَ	جَ	كَ	كَ	صَ	أ	ضَ	كَ

هَضَمَ	عَبَسَ
صَدَقَ	أَكَلَ
أَحَدَ	رَكَضَ
سَأَلَ	فَصَدَقَ
سَحَبَ	غَفَرَ
جَمَعَ	جَبَرَ

Exercise
Word Search

تَ	رَ	كَ	تَ	هَ	تَ	فَ	تَ	حَ
ظَ	طَ	عَ	ظَ	كَ	ظَ	كَ	جَ	سَ
عَ	تَ	رَ	تَ	عَ	ظَ	كَ	ثَ	دَ
رَ	ظَ	كَ	قَ	وَ	عَ	ظَ	مَ	تَ
ظَ	تَ	بَ	ظَ	كَ	رَ	ظَ	كَ	مَ
عَ	فَ	سَ	أَ	لَ	تَ	قَ	تَ	لَ
رَ	تَ	طَ	تَ	قَ	وَ	عَ	ظَ	كَ
وَ	رَ	دَ	عَ	ظَ	كَ	شَ	فَ	عَ

تَرَكَ	شَفَعَ
صَعَدَ	نَزَلَ
حَسَدَ	وَعَظَ
طَرَقَ	بَسَطَ
وَرَقَ	هَتَفَ
وَرَدَ	مَلَكَ

Exercise
Word Search

أَ	خَ	ذَ	صَ	بَ	بَ	جَ	لَ	سَ
هَ	صَ	بَ	بَ	جَ	لَ	سَ	تَ	رَ
هَ	بَ	صَ	بَ	رَ	هَ	بَ	جَ	لَ
جَ	لَ	حَ	دَ	صَ	بَ	نَ	هَ	رَ
رَ	صَ	بَ	سَ	قَ	بَ	سَ	بَ	هَ
صَ	بَ	حَ	هَ	دَ	لَ	بَ	لَ	لَ
فَ	تَ	حَ	صَ	بَ	جَ	لَ	سَ	مَ
صَ	بَ	هَ	نَ	صَ	رَ	حَ	هَ	سَ

أَخَذَ	سَتَرَ
هَجَرَ	مَسَكَ
نَهَرَ	حَسَدَ
فَتَحَ	نَسَبَ
صَبَرَ	جَلَسَ
نَصَرَ	لَمَسَ

Exercise
Word Search

دَ	بَ	رَ	ضَ	لَ	قَ	مَ	سَ	ق
هَ	وَ	فَ	عَ	قَ	فَ	لَ	دَ	عَ
سَ	وَ	فَ	وَ	فَ	فَ	وَ	لَ
مَ	تَ	جَ	صَ	فَ	قَ	ا	مَ	نَ
وَ	عَ	لَ	زَ	عَ	حَ	ا	زَ
قَ	وَ	عَ	جَ	وَ	فَ	وَ	عَ
فَ	صَ	ا	هَ	صَ	لَ	لَ	وَ
فَ	سَ	خَ	عَ	مَ	شَ	أ	دَ	صَ

لَمَح	قَسَم
صَدَأ	خَسَف
وَقَف	دَهَس
نَزَع	ضَرَب
شَمَع	وَصَل
خَتَم	عَدَل

Exercise
Word Search

بَ	تَ	لَ	بَ	حَ	ا	ضَ	رَ	ق
سَ	بَ	حَ	حَ	زَ	بَ	ا	سَ	سَ
طَ	ا	ظَ	جَ	دَ	سَ	مَ	ا	كَ
رَ	جَ	شَ	زَ	بَ	رَ	بَ	حَ	بَ
بَ	تَ	لَ	بَ	تَ	لَ	حَ	زَ	ا
بَ	بَ	حَ	سَ	بَ	حَ	زَ	بَ	طَ
بَ	حَ	سَ	فَ	حَ	زَ	ا	رَ	ا
فَ	قَ	وَ	شَ	مَ	عَ	فَ	طَ	خَ

قَسَم	قَرَض
وَقَف	خَطَب
مَسَد	بَسَط
لَحَظ	زَحَف
سَكَب	طَرَف
بَسَر	شَجَر

حَ	لَ	فَ	حَ	دَ	فَ	دَ	فَ	نَ
حَ	حَ	سَ	حَ	بَ	طَ	بَ	طَ	شَ
حَ	جَ	أَ	مَ	نَ	زَ	زَ	لَ	لَ
مَ	هَ	لَ	حَ	لَ	بَ	زَ	عَ	عَ
مَ	زَ	مَ	سَ	عَ	زَ	ضَ	ا	ا
دَ	فَ	بَ	طَ	حَ	جَ	أَ	مَ	مَ
بَ	طَ	نَ	جَ	مَ	هَ	لَ	حَ	حَ
نَ	جَ	حَ	جَ	زَ	مَ	أَ	مَ	رَ

أَمَرَ	حَلَفَ
جَلَسَ	فَسَأَلَ
بَطَشَ	دَفَنَ
نَجَحَ	أَمَنَ
نَبَضَ	طَلَعَ
جَهَزَ	جَزَمَ

Exercise
Word Search

نَ	رَ	كَ	سَ	مَ	كَ	ثَ	نَ	ذَ
صَ	بَ	رَ	ا	قَ	بَ	كَ	رَ	سَ
صَ	قَ	كَ	رَ	سَ	طَ	صَ	ضَ	كَ
دَ	كَ	رَ	سَ	ذَ	نَ	ذَ	رَ	ذَ
قَ	نَ	طَ	نَ	ذَ	طَ	ذَ	ذَ	شَ
قَ	قَ	حَ	نَ	ذَ	حَ	ضَ	كَ	غَ
قَ	طَ	قَ	ضَ	كَ	رَ	سَ	ا	لَ
ضَ	كَ	فَ	قَ	رَ	ا	كَ	رَ	سَ

نَذَرَ	نَكَرَ
صَدَقَ	قَنَطَ
شَغَلَ	حَضَرَ
صَبَرَ	بَصَرَ
سَقَطَ	نَطَحَ
قَطَفَ	مَكَثَ

67

darulqurra.org

القاعدة السمنودية للمبتدئين

Chapter Two

Introduction to Vowels

In this chapter, we will learn a new sound for each letter created by a kasrah (ِ) or a ḍammah (ُ)

- Recite without spelling and differentiate the sounds between each letter.
- Recite each letter short without an abrupt stop.

Examples of VOWEL SOUNDS					
Name of Vowel		Shape	Sound	Shape	Sound
Fatḥah	above	أَ	Apple	هَ	Happy
Kasrah	below	إِ	India	هِ	He
Ḍammah	above	أُ	Oops	هُ	Who

Hurūf Al Ḥalqiyyah

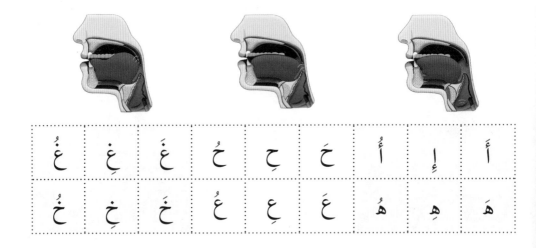

غُ	غِ	غَ	حُ	حِ	حَ	أُ	إِ	أَ
خُ	خِ	خَ	عُ	عِ	عَ	هُ	هِ	هَ

Hurūf Al Lahwiyyah

Remember to raise the back of the tongue to give a full mouth sound when reciting the letter قَ

اُكُ	اِكِ	اكَ	قُ	قِ	قَ

Hurūf Al Shajariyyah

Remember to keep the back of the tongue low to give an empty mouth sound in all of these letters.

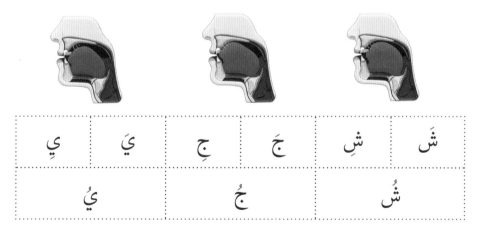

يِ	يَ	جِ	جَ	شِ	شَ
يُ		جُ		شُ	

Remember to raise the back of the tongue whilst forcing the sound of ضَ out from the middle left or right side of the tongue.

ضُ	ضِ	ضَ

Ḥurūf Al Thalqiyyah

Remember to lower the back of the tongue whilst reciting the letter (ر) with a kasra creating an empty mouth sound.

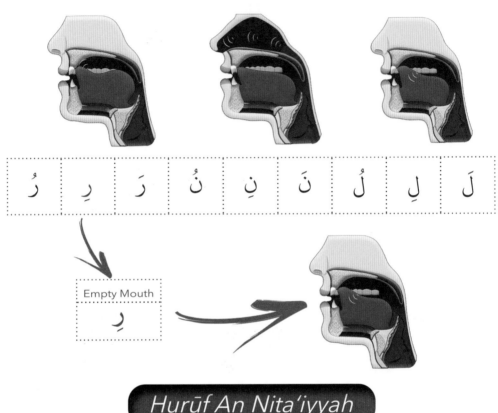

رُ | رِ | رَ | نُ | نِ | نَ | لُ | لِ | لَ

Empty Mouth

رِ

Ḥurūf An Niṭa'iyyah

By raising the back of the tongue whilst reciting the letter (ط) to create a full mouth sound.

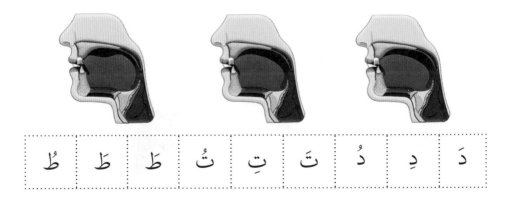

طُ | طِ | طَ | تُ | تِ | تَ | دُ | دِ | دَ

Hurūf Al Asliyyah

By raising the back of the tongue whilst reciting the letter ﺺ to create a full mouth sound.

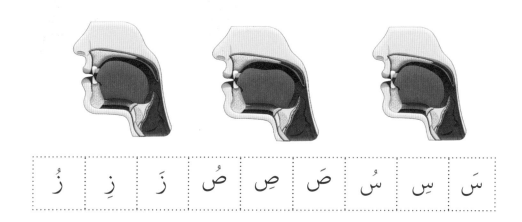

زُ	زِ	زَ	صُ	صِ	صَ	سُ	سِ	سَ

Hurūf Al Lithawiyyah

By raising the back of the tongue whilst reciting the letter ﻅ to create a full mouth sound.

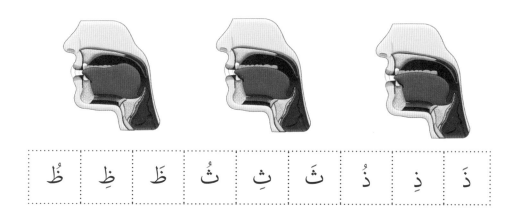

ظُ	ظِ	ظَ	ثُ	ثِ	ثَ	ذُ	ذِ	ذَ

Hurūf As Shafawiyyah

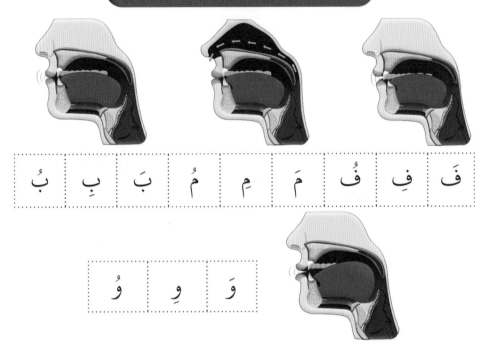

بُ	بِ	بَ	مُ	مَ	فُ	فَ

وُ	وِ	وَ

Lesson 2   Connecting Letters

In this lesson, concentrate on the shapes of letters and identify similarities between them whilst connecting with other letters to form short words.

- Continue without spelling and try to differentiate the sounds between each letter.

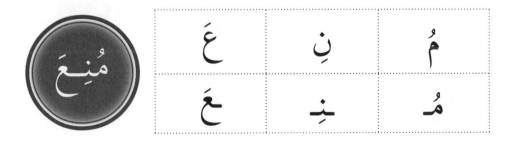

مُ	نِ	عَ
مُـ	ـنِـ	ـعَ

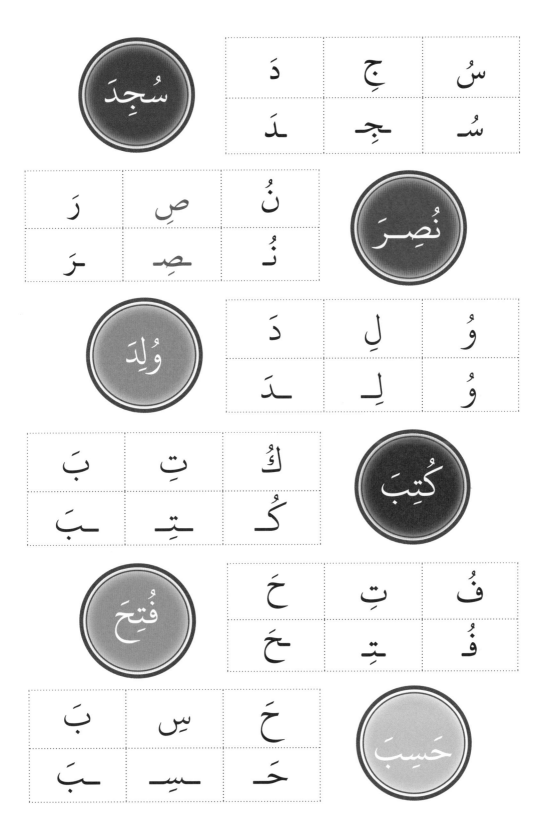

سُجِدَ — سُ جِ دَ / سُ جِ دَ

نُصِرَ — نُ صِ رَ / نُ صِ رَ

وُلِدَ — وُ لِ دَ / وُ لِ دَ

كُتِبَ — كُ تِ بَ / كُ تِ بَ

فُتِحَ — فُ تِ حَ / فُ تِ حَ

حَسِبَ — حَ سِ بَ / حَ سِ بَ

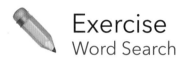

Exercise
Word Search

كُ	تِ	بَ	رِ	عُ	هِ	دَ	ضَ	نِ
حُ	نُ	رُ	لِ	سُ	كِ	نَ	لُ	خُ
لِ	نِ	وُ	ثُ	لُ	فُ	تِ	حَ	كُ
بَ	شِ	لِ	ثِ	شَ	هِ	دَ	طِ	دِ
يِ	يِ	هِ	حَ	سِ	بَ	فُ	خِ	خ
ثُ	رُ	مُ	نِ	عَ	كُ	ص	ح	بَ
مَ	سُ	وِ	نُ	صِ	رَ	م	ظَ	طَ
فُ	رَ	صُ	دَ	ذِ	سُ	ج	دَ	شَ

كُتِبَ	مُنِعَ
عُهِدَ	فُرِضَ
حَسِبَ	فُتِحَ
شَهِدَ	صَحِبَ
نُصِرَ	وُلِدَ
سُجِدَ	سُكِنَ

كُ	تِ	بَ	رِ	عُ	هِ	دَ	ضَ	نِ
حُ	نُ	رُ	لِ	سُ	كِ	نَ	لُ	خُ
لِ	شِ	أُ	كِ	لَ	فُ	وَ	رَ	قِ
نُ	شَ	رَ	عَ	م	لَ	دَ	طِ	دِ
خُ	بَ	زَ	هِ	حَ	سِ	بَ	فُ	خِ
ثُ	رُ	مُ	نِ	نُ	سِ	يَ	ح	غُ
قُ	تِ	لَ	مَ	ثُ	لُ	م	ظَ	لِ
لُ	طِ	فَ	دَ	مَ	لَ	كُ	دَ	بَ

حُشِرَ	أُكِلَ
نُسِيَ	غُلِبَ
عُهِدَ	خُبِزَ
لُطِفَ	مَلَكُ
عَمِلَ	وَرَقِ
قُتِلَ	مَثَلُ

Exercise
Word Search

فَتَحَ	وُلِدَ
رَكَعَ	هَتَفَ
هَضَمَ	حَلَفَ
غُلِبَ	عَبَسَ
قُرِأَ	وَنَخَلَ
فُتِحَ	دُخِلَ

قُ	لَ	خَ	نَ	وَ	قُ	حَ	تَ	فَ
فَ	لَ	حَ	لِ	وُ	قُ	وَ	فُ	قُ
شَ	شَ	شَ	بَ	لِ	رَ	تِ	وُ	وَ
فَ	تَ	هَ	شَ	دَ	كَ	لِ	حَ	وُ
نِ	لِ	ضَ	نِ	لِ	عَ	شَ	عَ	لِ
شَ	بَ	مَ	شَ	بَ	شَ	بَ	لِ	غُ
هَ	أَ	رِ	قُ	لِ	سَ	لِ	نِ	قُ
لَ	خِ	دُ	هَ	بَ	قُ	شَ	بَ	شَ

سُمِعَ	خُطِبَ
خَلَدَ	مَسَحَ
نَصَفَ	غَمَرَ
أَثَرَ	وَعَظَ
تَرَكَ	أُكِلَ
سُئِلَ	رَكَضَ

نَ	قُ	قُ	ضَ	كَ	رَ	عَ	مِ	سُ
صَ	شَ	بَ	مَ	شَ	بَ	شَ	بَ	رَ
فَ	هَ	أَ	رِ	قُ	لِ	سَ	نِ	غَ
رَ	لَ	خِ	دُ	هَ	قُ	قُ	مَ	وَ
دَ	لَ	خَ	شَ	بَ	طِ	رَ	أَ	عَ
سُ	حَ	سَ	مَ	ا	ا	ثَ	رَ	ظَ
إِ	لَ	خِ	دُ	هَ	رَ	لَ	كِ	أُ
لَ	شَ	كَ	رَ	تَ	شَ	بَ	طِ	خُ

In this lesson, continue concentrating on the shapes of letters and the sound.

- Continue without spelling and try to differentiate the sound between each letter.
- Recite each letter short without an abrupt stop.
- Remember to continue differentiating between full-mouth and empty mouth sounds.

شَهِدَ	دَ	هِ	شَ	حَسِبَ	بَ	سِ	حَ
	دَ	ـهِـ	ـشَـ		ـبَ	ـسِـ	حَـ
كَئِبَ	بَ	ءِ	كَ	عَمِلَ	لَ	مِ	عَ
	ـبَ	ـئِـ	كَ		ـلَ	ـمِ	عَـ
صَحِبَ	بَ	حِ	صَ	بَرِىَٔ	ىَٔ	رِ	بَ
	ـبَ	ـحِـ	صَـ		ىَٔ	ـرِ	بَـ
وَرَق	قِ	رَ	وَ	مِئَةَ	ةَ	ءَ	مِ
	قِ	رَ	وَ		ـةَ	ـئَـ	مِـ
عُهِدَ	دَ	هِ	عُ	مَثَلُ	لُ	ثَ	مَ
	ـدَ	ـهِـ	عُـ		ـلُ	ـثَ	مَـ

فُرصُ	صُ	رَ	فُ	أُكِلَ	لَ	كِ	أُ
	صُ	رَ	فُ		لَ	كِ	أُ
حُشِرَ	رَ	شُ	حُ	خُبِزَ	زَ	بِ	خُ
	رَ	شِ	حُ		نَ	بْ	خُ
شُهِدَ	دَ	هِ	شُ	غُلِبَ	بَ	لِ	غُ
	دَ	هِ	شُ		بْ	لِ	غُ
كُتِبَ	بَ	تِ	كُ	شُكِرَ	رَ	كِ	شُ
	بَ	تِ	كُ		رَ	كِ	شُ
نُسِيَ	يَ	سِ	نُ	قُتِلَ	لَ	تِ	قُ
	يَ	سِ	نُ		لَ	تِ	قُ
سُبُلُ	لُ	بُ	سُ	فُتِحَ	حَ	تِ	فُ
	لُ	بْ	سُ		حَ	تِ	فُ
رُسُلُ	لُ	سُ	رُ	مَثَلُ	لُ	ثَ	مَ
	لُ	سُ	رُ		لُ	ثْ	مَ

Remember to continue differentiating between full-mouth and empty mouth sounds.

نُهَض	ض هِ ض	نُ نُ	ضُرِبَ / بَ رِ ضُ	ضُ بَ رِ / ضُـ رِ بَـ
أُفْق	قُ ق قُ	أُ فُ / أُ فَ	لُطِفَ / لَطِفَ فَ	لَ طُ فَ / لُ طِـ فَـ

لَكُمُ	رَجُلُ	فَهُوَ	سُبُلُ	سَأَلَكَ
صُحُفِ	هُدِىَ	سُقِطَ	عُصِمَ	لَهُمْ
نُصِبَ	وُقِعَ	أُفِكَ	غُفِرَ	مَثَلُ
أَعِظْكَ	فَبَصَرُكَ	وَيَهَبُ	لَقُضِىَ	أَصِلُ
حُمِلَ	رَحِمَهُ	ذُبِحَ	قَوِىَ	فَغَفَرَلَه
كُسِرَ	فَقُتِلَ	كَذِبَ	وَرَقُكَ	فَهُدِىَ
رُتِبَ	جُمِعَ	حُفِظَ	زُرِعَ	خُلِقَ
غُضِبَ	سُلِمَ	فَدُفِعَ	أَحَدُكُمْ	ذُكِرَ

نُقِلَ	حُجَرُ	عُقَدُ	لُطُفَ	سُدُسُهُ
فَنُصِرَ	وَلَدُهُ	سُرُرَهُ	فُرُشَهُ	عُمَرُ
وَيَقِفُ	وَقَفَ	وَخُلِعَ	رَضِىَ	كَرُمَ
فُتِحَ	ثُبِّتَ	رَؤُفَ	نَظُفَ	قُرِئَ
دُخِلَ	طُرِقَ	أُكِلَ	حَسُنَ	غُلِبَتِ
لُبِسَ	أَحَدَ	سُئِلَ	مَلِكَ	فَهُدِى
وُرِدَ	وُلِدَ	نُجِحَ	جَمُلَ	خُلُقُهُ
فَضَعُفَ	وَوُجِدَ	كُتِبَ	وَيَزِنُ	وَزَنَ
ضُرِبَ	فُعِلَ	بُهِتَ	أُذِنَ	رُسِمَ
هُدِىَ	مُنِعَ	عُتِقَ	فُتِحَ	نُصِرَ
فَحُشِرَ	حُشِرَ	نَبُؤُهُ	خُمُسَهُ	فَغُضِبَ
ظُلِمَ	بِقَلَمِهِ	جُرِحَ	فَخَشَعَ	وَقُسِمَ
ضُبِطَ	مَلَكَ	أَدَبُهُ	فَدُخِلَ	ظُلِمَ
بَلَدِ	قَلَمَ	فَعَدَلَكَ	فَفَسَقَ	يَهَبُ
صُبِرَ	نَزَغَ	إِرَمَ	فَقَدَرَ	مَلَكَ
وَخُلُقُ	خُرِجَ	لِيَصِلَ	سَمِعَ	بُعِثَ

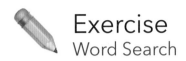

Exercise
Word Search

فَ	عَ	دَ	لَ	كَ	قُ	كَ	ذِ	بَ
لَ	قُ	ضِ	ىَ	سُ	مِ	نَ	لُ	خُ
كُ	نِ	وُ	ثُ	لُ	أَ	عِ	ظُ	كَ
سِ	شَ	لِ	ثِ	شَ	هِ	أَ	صِ	لُ
رَ	ي	سَ	أَ	لَ	كَ	بَ	فُ	خِ
تُ	رُ	مُ	نِ	عَ	كُ	رَ	جُ	لُ
فَ	غَ	فَ	رَ	لَ	هُ	مِ	ظَ	طَ
فَ	فَ	سَ	قَ	ذِ	يَ	هَ	بُ	شَ

فَفَسَقَ	يَهَبُ	فَعَدَلَكَ	قُمِ	كَذِبَ	لَقُضِىَ
كُسِرَ	فَغَفَرَلَهُ	أَصِلُ	رَجُلُ	أَعِظُكَ	سَأَلَكَ

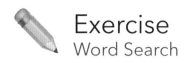

Exercise
Word Search

وَ	قُ	سِ	مَ	عُ	هِ	دَ	ضَ	طُ
حُ	نُ	رُ	لِ	يَ	صِ	لَ	وَ	رِ
خُ	لُ	قُ	هُ	لَ	فُ	وَ	خُ	قَ
نُ	وَ	يَ	قِ	فُ	لَ	دَ	لُ	رِ
سُ	دُ	سُ	هُ	وُ	وَ	خُ	لِ	عَ
تُ	رُ	مُ	نِ	لِ	وَ	خُ	لُ	قُ
فُ	عِ	لَ	مَ	دَ	عُ	تِ	قَ	لِ
لُ	طِ	فَ	دَ	مَ	لُ	طُ	فُ	بَ

وَيَقِفْ	خُلُقُهُ	وَخُلُقُ	لِيَصِلَ	وَقُسِمَ	طُرِقَ
لُطُفْ	عُتِقَ	فُعِلَ	وُلِدَ	وَخُلِعَ	سُدُسُهُ

Exercise
Word Search

صَ	ضَ	فَ	قَ	وَ	رِ	مَ	سَ	قَ		
دَ	لُ	نَ	كِ	زَ	لَ	رُ	خَ	حُ	لَمَح	قَسَم
أ	طَ	بِ	جَ	مَ	ثُ	سَ	رَ	نَ	صَدَأ	خَسَف
ثَ	طِ	رَ	حَ	شَ	فَ	مَ	أ	طَ	وَقَف	دَهَس
دَ	ةَ	ئَ	مَ	تَ	خَ	سَ	فَ	حَ	نَزَع	كَسَر
هَ	حِ	لَ	كُ	عَ	نِ	مِ	رُ	رِ	زَجَر	نَطَح
سَ	بِ	مِ	عَ	زَ	نَ	وِ	سُ	بَ	خَتَم	عَدَل
لَ	دَ	عَ	طِ	وَ	دَ	رَ	سَ	كَ		

Exercise
Word Search

نِ	ضَ	عَ	بِ	شَ	رِ	بَ	تَ	كَ		
خُ	لُ	نَ	كِ	سُ	لِ	رُ	ذَ	حُ	رِئَة	أَثَرِ
أ	طَ	بِ	حَ	لُ	ثُ	وُ	رَ	لِ	لَبِس	وَطِئَ
ثَ	طِ	دَ	هِ	شَ	ثِ	مَ	أ	زَ	حَبِط	شَبِع
رِ	ةَ	ئَ	رِ	حَ	هِ	فَ	سَ	جَ	سَمِن	جَرِب
بَ	حِ	لَ	كُ	عَ	نِ	مِ	كَ	رِ	كَرُم	زَأَم
طَ	بِ	مِ	رَ	صِ	نَ	رُ	سُ	بَ	ذَرَأ	كَتَب
سَ	دَ	ئَ	طِ	وَ	مَ	ضُ	رَ	فُ		

Exercise
Word Search

بَ	كِ	نَ	زِ	حَ	رِ	لَ	خِ	بَ	
سِ	خِ	لِ	كِ	سُ	فَ	لِ	أَ	مِ	صِفَة — بَخِلَ
مَ	رَ	وَ	مَ	لَ	كِ	أُ	ئَ	لِ	غَنَم — فَسَأَل
ةَ	بَ	هِ	لَ	مِ	عَ	ةَ	شَ	نُ	أَلِف — هِيَ
خِ	فُ	مِ	نَ	غَ	هِ	زَ	صِ	خُ	بَسَط — بَسِمَ
غُ	حِ	يَ	سِ	نُ	يَ	مُ	فَ	ثُ	حَزِنَ — مِئَة
لِ	لَ	أَ	سَ	فَ	مَ	لَ	ةَ	قُ	هِبَة — مَلِك
طَ	سَ	بَ	لَ	لَ	خِ	بَ	طِ	لُ	

Exercise
Word Search

دَ	سَ	حَ	أَ	أَ	أَ	قَ	قَ	سَ	
لَ	لَ	قَ	قَ	سَ	لَ	جَ	قَ	سَ	سَتَر — أَخَذَ
صَ	نَ	لَ	تَ	قَ	أَ	ذَ	خَ	أَ	صَدَق — هَجَرَ
بَ	صَ	رَ	هَ	قَ	دَ	صَ	أَ	أَ	حَسَد — خَلَق
رَ	رَ	جَ	دَ	سَ	دَ	قَ	قَ	قَ	جَمَع — فَتَح
دَ	رَ	أَ	أَ	دَ	جَ	وَ	جَ	جَ	جَلَس — صَبَر
لَ	حَ	تَ	فَ	جَ	مَ	لَ	جَ	لَ	وَجَد — نَصَر
قَ	قَ	لَ	أَ	جَ	عَ	قَ	لَ	خَ	

SCAN ME

darulqurra.org

القاعدة السمنودية للمبتدئين

Chapter Three
Introduction to Madd Aṣlī
(Prolongation)

In this lesson, we will discuss a special letter called Alif

Some Special Facts about Alif:

- Alif always stretches the sound of the letter before it.
- Alif will never have a vowel (Ḥarakah).
- Alif is always written alone or joined with the letter before it but never joins the letter after it.
- Alif is also known as Alif Saghīrah or a vertical fatḥah if it appears above another letter.

مٰ

	Read with a long sound (2 Ḥarakah)	Read with a short sound (1 Ḥarakah)
Remember the addition of Alif will <u>double</u> the duration of sound	اَء	ءَ
	هَا	هَ
	حَا	حَ
Alif will be recited with a full mouth sound if it follows a full mouth letter	عَا	عَ
	غَا	غَ
	خَا	خَ

Long sound (2 Ḥarakah)	Short sound
قَا	قَ
كَا	كَ
شَا	شَ
جَا	جَ
يَا	يَ

Long sound (2 Ḥarakah)	Short sound
ضَا	ضَ
لَا	لَ
نَا	نَ
رَا	رَ

Long sound (2 Ḥarakah)	Short sound
دَا	دَ
تَا	تَ
طَا	طَ

Long sound (2 Ḥarakah)	Short sound
فَا	فَ
مَا	مَ
بَا	بَ
وَا	وَ

Long sound (2 Ḥarakah)	Short sound
سَا	سَ
صَا	صَ
زَا	زَ

Long sound (2 Ḥarakah)	Short sound
ثَا	ثَ
ذَا	ذَ
ظَا	ظَ

Long	Short	Long	Short	Long	Short	Long	Short
عَا	عَ	حَا	حَ	هَا	هَ	ءَا	ءَ
كَا	كَ	قَا	قَ	خَا	خَ	غَا	غَ
ضَا	ضَ	يَا	يَ	جَا	جَ	شَا	شَ
دَا	دَ	رَا	رَ	نَا	نَ	لَا	لَ
صَا	صَ	سَا	سَ	طَا	طَ	تَا	تَ
ظَا	ظَ	ذَا	ذَ	ثَا	ثَ	زَا	زَ
وَا	وَ	بَا	بَ	مَا	مَ	فَا	فَ

Exercise
Word Search

هَا	ضَ	دَ	هَ	دَا	يَا	سِ	قُ	غَا
جَ	عَا	عَ	حَا	حَ	هَا	هَ	مَ	حُ
رَ	ءَا	كَ	سَ	قَ	خَا	رَ	لُ	خُ
رِ	مَ	ضَ	دَ	يَ	جَا	جَ	وَ	نُ
عَ	نَ	دَ	رَا	رَ	نَا	نَ	سَ	حَا
غُ	صَا	صَ	سَا	سَ	طَا	طَ	رُ	بَ
لِ	دَ	بَ	عَا	ذَ	ثَا	بَ	لَ	غَا
بَ	فُ	طُ	لُ	مَ	مَ	دَ	ءِ	غَا

حَاسَدَ	هَاجَرَ
عَابَدَ	اِدَمَ
غَامَرَ	ءَامَنَ
غَالَبَ	حَاسَنَ

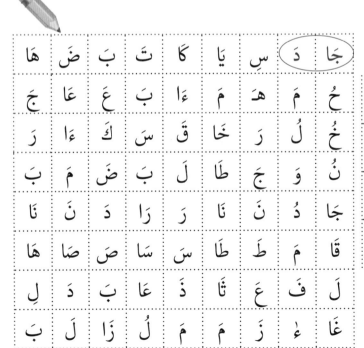

هَا	ضَ	بَ	تَ	كَا	يَا	سِ	دَ	جَا
جَ	عَا	عَ	بَ	ءَا	مَ	هَ	مَ	حُ
رَ	ءَا	كَ	سَ	قَ	خَا	رَ	لُ	خُ
بَ	مَ	ضَ	بَ	لَ	طَا	جَ	وَ	نُ
نَا	نَ	دَ	رَا	رَ	نَا	نَ	دُ	جَا
هَا	صَا	صَ	سَا	سَ	طَا	طَ	مَ	قَا
لِ	دَ	بَ	عَا	ذَ	ثَا	عَ	فَ	لَ
بَ	لَ	زَا	لُ	مَ	مَ	زَ	ءِ	غَا

جَادَ	زَالَ
كَاتَبَ	مَءَابَ
جَامَعَ	قَافَزَ
بَنَاهَا	طَالَبَ

Revision 3.1 📖

Remember to continue reciting without spelling and differentiating the sound between full and empty mouth, short and long letters clearly.

عَارَض	نَاهَر	غَالَب	هَاجَر	ءَادَم
قَارَض	جَالَس	مَاسَح	حَاسَد	خَاف
فَاسَد	فَارَش	غَامَر	حَاسَن	زَال
رَاكَب	شَامَع	وَاعَظَ	مَاذَا	قَالَتَا
مَامَا	نَام	مَال	جَاد	أَصَابَهَا
طَالَب	مَئَاب	دَعَانَا	فَاق	أَمَام
وَارَد	تَوَابَل	نَاجَح	هَامَس	سَاخَط
بَاسَط	ثَابَت	كَاتَب	نَاقَص	تَوَابَا
نَاظَر	وَاعَد	وَاعَظَ	عَابَد	بَيَان
أَفَلَا	جَامَع	قَاتَل	غَارَس	قَافَز
سَلَام	خَلَقَا	بَنَاهَا	مَالَهَا	لَهَا
فَتَحَا	أَقَام	صَوَابَهَا	فَقَتَلَا	حَرَام

Lesson 2 Small Alif

In this lesson, we will look at the small Alif that sits above the letters but is recited just like the full size Alif with a two Ḥarakah length.

	Small Alif	Small Alif	Alif	Length
Empty Mouth	ءٰ	ءَٰ	ءَا	2 Ḥarakah
Empty Mouth	هـٰ	هَـٰ	هَا	2 Ḥarakah
Empty Mouth	حـٰ	حَـٰ	حَا	2 Ḥarakah
Empty Mouth	عـٰ	عَـٰ	عَـا	2 Ḥarakah
Full Mouth	غـٰ	غَـٰ	غَـا	2 Ḥarakah
Full Mouth	خـٰ	خَـٰ	خَا	2 Ḥarakah

Revision 3.2 📖

Remember to continue reciting without spelling and differentiating the sound between full and empty mouth, short and long letters clearly.

عَارَض	تَلَـٰهَا	صَلَوٰة	ءَادَمَ	ءْدَمَ
تَعَالَىٰ	دَحْهَا	دَحَهَا	هَاجَرَ	هَدْنَا
ءَامَنَ	يَتَمَىٰ	غَامَرَ	فَهَدَىٰ	زَالَ
رَاكَب	شَامَعَ	مَاهَـٰذَا	هَـٰذَا	هَـٰذَا
سَلَمَ	فَتَاوىٰ	ءَايَتَ	نَصَرىٰ	أَصَبَهَا
طَالَب	مَئَاب	فَتْـٰهَا	تَمَارَىٰ	أَمَامَ
وَارَدَ	فَنَادَىٰ	دَعَا	سَعَىٰ	أَتَـٰكَ
تَخَافَا	وَقَالَ	تَظْهَرَا	نَاقَصَ	دَحَاهَا
تَقَارَبَا	وَاعَدَ	عَامَرَ	عَابَدَ	بَيَانَ
تَسَالَهَا	قَضَاهَا	قَاتَلَ	تَفَاهَمَا	سَحَابَ
يَرَىٰ	خَلَقَنَا	بَنْـٰهَا	مَالَهَا	لَهَا
عَلَىٰ	أَقَامَ	جَاهَدَ	طَاقَ	هَدَايَا

In this lesson, we will discuss another special letter called Yā Sākinah which also lengthens the sound of the letter that comes before it with a kasra.

Some Special Facts of Yā Sākinah:

- Yā Sākinah stretches the sound of the letter before it.

- Yā Sākinah will never have a vowel or be read on its own.

- Yā Sākinah can be written alone or joined with the letters before or after it.

	Yā Sākinah read with a long sound (2 Ḥarakah)	Yā Sākinah read with a long sound (2 Ḥarakah)	Read with short sound	Length
	Both recited identically with 2 Ḥarakah			
Empty Mouth	إِي	إِيْ	ءِ	2 Ḥarakah
Empty Mouth	هِي	هِيْ	هِ	2 Ḥarakah
Empty Mouth	حِي	حِيْ	حِ	2 Ḥarakah
Empty Mouth	عِي	عِيْ	عِ	2 Ḥarakah
Full Mouth	غِي	غِيْ	غِ	2 Ḥarakah
Full Mouth	خِي	خِيْ	خِ	2 Ḥarakah

Long sound (2 Ḥarakah)	Long sound (2 Ḥarakah)	Short sound
قِي	قِيْ	قِ
كِي	كِيْ	كِ
شِي	شِيْ	شِ
جِي	جِيْ	جِ
يِي	يِيْ	يِ

Long sound (2 Ḥarakah)	Long sound (2 Ḥarakah)	Short sound
ضِي	ضِيْ	ضِ
لِي	لِيْ	لِ
نِي	نِيْ	نِ
رِي	رِيْ	رِ

Long sound (2 Ḥarakah)	Long sound (2 Ḥarakah)	Short sound
دِي	دِيْ	دِ
تِي	تِيْ	تِ
طِي	طِيْ	طِ

Long sound (2 Ḥarakah)	Long sound (2 Ḥarakah)	Short sound
سِي	سِيْ	سِ
صِي	صِيْ	صِ
زِي	زِيْ	زِ

Long sound (2 Ḥarakah)	Long sound (2 Ḥarakah)	Short sound
ثِي	ثِيْ	ثِ
ذِي	ذِيْ	ذِ
ظِي	ظِيْ	ظِ

Long sound (2 Ḥarakah)	Long sound (2 Ḥarakah)	Short sound
فِي	فِيْ	فِ
مِي	مِيْ	مِ
بِي	بِيْ	بِ
وِي	وِيْ	وِ

ءِ	ئِي	هِ	زِي	حِ	حِي	ع	عِي
غِ	غِي	خ	خِي	قِ	قِي	ك	كِي
شِ	شِي	ج	جِي	ي	يِي	ضِ	ضِي
لِ	لِي	ن	نِي	رِ	رِي	د	دِي
تِ	تِي	طِ	طِي	سِ	سِي	ص	صِي
زِ	زِي	ثِ	ثِي	ذِ	ذِي	ظِ	ظِي
فِ	فِي	م	مِي	بِ	بِي	و	وِي

Exercise
Word Search

ا	بَ	ا	ئِي	كِ	أ	لُ	ثِ ئِي
ا	ظَ	ئِي	رِ	لُ	ا	ا	ثُ وَ
ئِي	لِ	ثَ	ا	ي	فِ	ا	زِ ئِي
ثُ	حُ	ا	كَ	و	دَ	شُ	ا تُ
ا	ضَ	ي	صِ	غُ	ا	أ	ا بَ
ي	م	ي	ج	ا	خَ	مُ	ي شِ
ا	سُ	تِ	تَ	ا	رَ	صِ	ا مُ
ا	ئِي	وِ	يَ	ا	ي	طِ	جُ لَ

ثِي	كِي
رِي	فِي
زِي	جِي
لِي	مِي
صِي	طِي
وِي	شِي

Revision 3.3

Remember to continue reciting without spelling and differentiating between the full and empty mouth sounds, short and long letters clearly.

حَكِيْم	سَمِيْع	حَفِيْظَ	مِيْلَادِ	خَاشِعِيْنَ
مِيْعَادَ	لَاعِبَ	نَذِيْرَ	بَشِيْرَ	صَغِيْرَ
سَالِكِيْن	بِيَمِيْنِ	فِيْهَا	فِيْهِ	قَالَ
حَسِيْبَ	خَبِيْرَ	لَطِيْفَ	أَبِيْهِ	مَسَاكِيْنَ
بِضَنِيْنِ	حَدِيْثَ	أَحَادِيْثَ	فِي دِيْنِ	مَرِيْضَ
غَنَمى	لَبِثِيْنَ	شَيْطِيْنَ	حَافِظِيْنَ	ظَالِمِيْنَ
أَبَابِيْلَ	سَبِيْلَ	شَهِيْدَ	عِبَادِى	عَظِيْمَ
تَبِيْدَ	عِزِيْنَ	وَسِيْقَ	فَكِهِيْنَ	فَرِحِيْنَ
مَحَارِيْبَ	أَخِى	زَارَنِى	سَهِيْلَةَ	قِيْلَ
ذَ ٰلِكَ	فَعَسَى	سِيْرَتَهَا	كُلِّى	مَقَالِيْدَ
خَمِدِيْنَ	عَالِمِيْنَ	ءَامِنِيْنَ	فَرِيْقَانِ	سَبِيْلِى
دِيْوَانِى	فِدَاءِى	فَكِهِيْنَ	عَشِيْرَتَكَ	سَفِلِيْنَ

In this lesson, practice between the short and long sounds

Continue concentrating on the entire word.

- Yā Sākinah can also appear in a very small form known as Yā Saghīrah or a small Alif under the letter recited long with two Ḥarakah.
(بِهٖ or بِهۦ)

ـهِۦ	ـهٖ	ـهِۦ	هٖى

Compare		Compare	
وَقِيلِهٖ	وَقِيلِهۦ	وَنَئَا بِجَانِبِهٖ	وَنَئَا بِجَانِبِهۦ
شِيعَتِهٖ	شِيعَتِهۦ	بِهٖ	بِهۦ
لِصَٰحِبِهٖ	لِصَٰحِبِهۦ	إِلَفِ	إِۦلَفِ
عَمَلِهٖ	عَمَلِهۦ	وَكُتُبِهٖ	وَكُتُبِهۦ
هَٰذِهٖ	هَٰذِهۦ	صَاحِبَتِهٖ	صَاحِبَتِهۦ
وَكُتُبِهٖ	وَكُتُبِهۦ	وَءَاخِرِهٖ	وَءَاخِرِهۦ
وَرُسُلِهٖ	وَرُسُلِهۦ	وَعِبَادَتِهٖ	وَعِبَادَتِهۦ
بِيَمِينِهٖ	بِيَمِينِهۦ	قَلَمِهٖ	قَلَمِهۦ
بِهٖ	بِهۦ	سَبِيلِهٖ	سَبِيلِهۦ
		بِشَمَالِهٖ	بِشَمَالِهۦ

Exercise
Word Search

غَ	ضَ	دَ	ا	ةَ	بَ	ا	صَ	أ
ا	صَ	قَ	ا	نَ	لِ	رُ	نُ	حُ
رَ	خُ	وَ	نَ	ا	يَ	بَ	أَ	قَ
سَ	طَ	مَ	ا	رَ	حَ	ئَ	قَ	ا
عَ	ا	خُ	وَ	هُ	سُ	ا	فَ	
غُ	لَ	رَ	ظَ	ا	نَ	مُ	زَ	مَ
لِ	بَ	تِ	عُ	رَ	مَ	ا	غَ	فُ
ضَ	رَ	ا	عَ	مَ	سَ	مَ	ا	ةَ

هَامَس	أَصَابَهَا
أَقَام	حَرَام
بَيَان	نَاقَص
طَالَب	نَاظَر
غَارَس	قَافَز
عَارَض	غَامَر

لَ	ا	قَ	نَ	ئَ	عِ	ا	شِ	خَ
حَ	عَ	فَ	سَ	نَ	رَ	ئَ	بِ	خَ
ا	ا	كِ	ا	نِ	ئَ	مِ	ئَ	بِ
فِ	لِ	هِ	فِ	ئَ	نِ	رَ	ا	زَ
ظِ	مِ	ئَ	لِ	ةَ	لَ	ئَ	هِ	سَ
ئَ	ئَ	نَ	ئَ	ا	نَ	مُ	زَ	زَ
نَ	نَ	نَ	تِ	رَ	هِ	ئَ	بِ	أَ
ضَ	رَ	ا	ثَ	ئَ	دِ	ا	حَ	أَ

قَالَ	خَاشِعِينَ
أَبِيهِ	أَحَادِيثَ
سَهِيلَةَ	حَافِظِينَ
بِيَمِينِ	خَبِيرَ
زَارَنِي	سَفِلِينَ
عَالِمِينَ	فَكِهِينَ

In this lesson, we will discuss another special letter called Waw Sākinah that helps lengthen the sound of the letter that comes before it with a ḍammah.

Some Special Facts of Waw Sākinah:

- Waw Sākinah always adapts the sound of the letter before it.
- Waw Sākinah will never have a vowel or be read on its own.
- Waw Sākinah is used to lengthen the sound of other letters.
- Waw Sākinah can be written alone or joined with the letters before but not after it.
- Waw Sākinah can appear with or without a physical Sakūn and in both scenarios will be recited identical.

	Waw Sākinah read with a long sound (2 Ḥarakah)	Waw Sākinah read with a long sound (2 Ḥarakah)	Read with short sound
	Both recited identically with 2 Ḥarakah		
Empty Mouth	أُو	أُوْ	ءُ
Empty Mouth	هُو	هُوْ	هُ
Empty Mouth	حُو	حُوْ	حُ
Empty Mouth	عُو	عُوْ	عُ
Full Mouth	غُو	غُوْ	غُ
Full Mouth	خُو	خُوْ	خُ

Long sound (2 Ḥarakah)	Long sound (2 Ḥarakah)	Short sound
قُو	قُوْ	قُ
كُو	كُوْ	اُك
شُو	شُوْ	شُ
جُو	جُوْ	جُ
يُو	يُوْ	يُ

Long sound (2 Ḥarakah)	Long sound (2 Ḥarakah)	Short sound
ضُو	ضُوْ	ضُ
لُو	لُوْ	لُ
نُو	نُوْ	نُ
رُو	رُوْ	رُ

Long sound (2 Ḥarakah)	Long sound (2 Ḥarakah)	Short sound
دُو	دُوْ	دُ
تُو	تُوْ	تُ
طُو	طُوْ	طُ

Long sound (2 Ḥarakah)	Long sound (2 Ḥarakah)	Short sound
سُو	سُوْ	سُ
صُو	صُوْ	صُ
زُو	زُوْ	زُ

Long sound (2 Ḥarakah)	Long sound (2 Ḥarakah)	Short sound
ثُو	ثُوْ	ثُ
ذُو	ذُوْ	ذُ
ظُو	ظُوْ	ظُ

Long sound (2 Ḥarakah)	Long sound (2 Ḥarakah)	Short sound
فُو	فُوْ	فُ
مُو	مُوْ	مُ
بُو	بُوْ	بُ
وُو	وُوْ	وُ

عُوْ	عُ	خُوْ	حُ	هُوْ	هُ	ئُوْ	أُ
كُوْ	كُ	قُوْ	قُ	خُوْ	خُ	غُوْ	غُ
ضُوْ	ضُ	يُوْ	يُ	جُوْ	جُ	شُوْ	شُ
دُوْ	دُ	رُوْ	رُ	نُوْ	نُ	لُوْ	لُ
صُوْ	صُ	سُوْ	سُ	طُوْ	طُ	تُوْ	تُ
ظُوْ	ظُ	ذُوْ	ذُ	ثُوْ	ثُ	زُوْ	زُ
وُوْ	وُ	بُوْ	بُ	مُوْ	مُ	فُوْ	فُ

Exercise
Word Search

ت	بَ	وْ	نُ	سْ	أَ	لُ	وْ	كُ	
وْ	ظُ	فَ	سَ	لُ	فَ	وْ	ثُ	مُوْ	كُوْ
ئ	لْ	ثُ	وْ	هُـ	زْ	أُ	ئَ	سْ	غُوْ	ذُوْ
تُ	حُ	ءِ	بُّ	و	عُ	شُ	وْ	تُ	جُوْ	نُوْ
وْ	ذُ	ئَ	و	غُ	سْ	أَ	لَ	كُ	هُوْ	تُوْ
نَ	نْ	دُ	طَ	وْ	مُ	مُ	مَ	دَا	ظُوْ	سُوْ
وْ	سُ	تِ	تِ	ا	رَ	صِ	قُ	مُ	ثُوْ	قُوْ
دِ	سِ	ا	هَـ	لْ	ضْ	وَ	جُ	لَ		

Lesson 6 Connecting letters of Madd

In this lesson, practice between the short and long sounds

- Waw Sākinah can also appear in a very small form known as Waw Saghīrah or a small vertical Ḍammah and both will be recited the same.
(ـهُۥ) or (ـهٗ)

Small vertical dammah	Waw Saghīrah	Small vertical dammah	Waw Saghīrah
كِتَٰبَهٗ	كِتَٰبَهُۥ	مَعَهٗ	مَعَهُۥ
مَثَلُهٗ	مَثَلُهُۥ	لَهٗ	لَهُۥ
وَجَعَلَهٗ	وَجَعَلَهُۥ	صَٰحِبُهٗ	صَٰحِبُهُۥ
مَالُهٗ	مَالُهُۥ	عَمَلُهٗ	عَمَلُهُۥ

عَمَلُهُۥ	حَافِظِينَ	وَنُسُكِي	سَأَلَكَ
كِتَٰبَهٗ	سُقِطَ	وَجَعَلَهُۥ	أُتِيتُهُۥ
وُقِعَ	مَثَلُهُۥ	وَثَاقَهُۥ	مَعَهُۥ
فَبَصَرُكَ	وَرَسُولَهُۥ	لَقُضِيَ	مَالُهٗ
وَرَسُولَهٗ	تَظَٰهَرَا	قَوِىَ	لَنُذِيقَهُۥ
فَقُتِلَ	مَوَازِينُهٗ	وَقِيلِهِۦ	فَهُدَىٰ
إِلَٰفِ	لَهُۥ	وَجَعَلَهٗ	سَبِيلِهِۦ
وَنَـَٔا بِجَانِبِهِۦ	عَمَلُهٗ	أَحَدُكُمُ	ذُكِرَ
فَخَلَقَهٗ	مَثَلُهٗ	فَخَلَقَهُۥ	مَوَازِينُهُۥ
أُتِيتَهٗ	صُحُفِ	بِهِۦ	وَكُتُبِهِۦ
قَلَمِهٖ	وَءَاخِرِهِۦ	شِيعَتِهِۦ	بِشِمَالِهٖ

Exercise
Connect the matching words.

مَالُهُ	مَثَلُهُ
وَجَعَلَهُ	وَجَعَلَهُ
مَعَهُ	كِتَبُهُ
مَثَلُهُ	مَالُهُ
عَمَلُهُ	صَـٰحِبُهُ
مَوَازِينُهُ	مَعَهُ
كِتَبَهُ	عَمَلُهُ
صَـٰحِبُهُ	لَهُ
لَهُ	مَوَازِينُهُ

Exercise
Word Search

يَ	ضِ	قُ	لَ	فَ خَ لَ قَ هـ			
هُ	لُ	مَ	عَ	نَ	رَ	يْ	بِ	فَ
لَ	هُ	قُ	ذِ	نُ	لَ	يَ	هُ
هُ	لِ	كَ	رُ	صَ	بَ	فَ	دِ
هِ	بِ	تُ	كُ	وَ	لَ	يَ	ىَ
يَ	هُ	تُ	يْ	تِ	أُ	مُ	مَ	كَ
لَ	تِ	قُ	فَ	رَ	هـ	بَ	تْ	كِ
ضَ	رَ	ا	رِ	خَ	ا	ءَ	وَ

وَكُتُبِهِ	فَخَلَقَهُ
كِتَبُهُ	لَقُضِيَ
لَهُ	فَقُتِلَ
فَهْدِيَ	لَنُذِيقَهُ
عَمَلُهُ	وَءَاخِرِهِ
فَبَصَرُكَ	أُتِيتُهُ

Exercise
Word Search

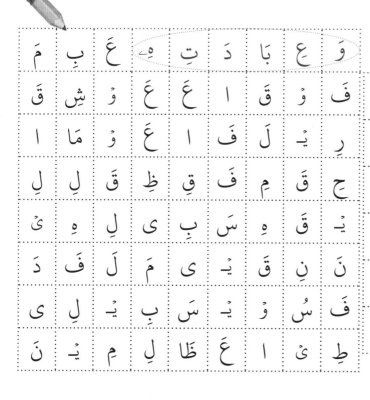

Word list (first puzzle):

فَقُتِلَ	حَافِظِينَ
بِشِمَالِهِ	أَحَدُكُمُ
سَأَلَكَ	وَثَاقَهُ
وَنُسُكِي	فَبَصَرُكَ
لَهُ	إِلْفِ
وَرُسُلِهِ	هَذِهِ

Word list (second puzzle):

ظَالِمِينَ	وَعِبَادَتِهِ
عَظِيمَ	قَلَمِهِ
فَرِحِينَ	سَبِيلِهِ
قِيلَ	بِشِمَالِهِ
مَقَالِيدَ	طِيٓ
سَبِيلِي	سُوٓ

Exercise
Word Search

ا	فَ	ا	خَ	تَ	مَ	مَ	لَ	سَ
دِ	لَ	تَ	تَ	أَ	دَ	ئِ	هِ	شَ
دِ	زَ	سَ	قَ	حَ	زَ	ئِيْ	يْ	
دِ	ا	ا	ا	ا	ا	طِ	ا	طِ
لَ	رَ	لَ	دِ	زَ	رَ	ئِيْ	ئِيْ	
طِ	نِ	هَ	بَ	ئِ	ا	طِ	نِ	نِ
ئِ	ئِ	ا	ا	ثَ	قَ	ئِ	سِ	وَ
فَ	بَ	لَ	ا	طَ	دَ	رَ	ا	وَ

سَلَمَ	لَطِيْفَ
طَالَبَ	أَحَادِيْثَ
وَارَدَ	شَيْطِيْنَ
تَخَافَا	شَهِيْدَ
تَقَارَبَا	وَسِيْقَ
تَسَالَهَا	زَارَنِي

لْ	نَ	ئِ	زِ	ى	تِ	ا	لَ	صَ
بْ	ئِ	شِ	عَ	هِٕ	نَ	ئِ	زِ	عَ
ثِ	لْ	كَ	تَ	رَ	ئِ	شِ	عَ	سَ
ئِ	لْ	نِ	ا	قَ	ئِ	رِ	فَ	هِ
نَ	ئِ	هِ	كِ	فَ	فِ	حُ	صُ	ئِ
نَ	ئِ	زِ	لْ	كُ	أَ	هِٕ	لَ	
ئِ	شِ	عَ	لْ	لِ	خِ	هِٕ	لْ	ةَ
لَ	ئِ	بَ	ى	دِ	ا	بَ	عِ	

صَلَاتِي	عِبَادِى
لِبِثِيْنَ	فَكِهِيْنَ
سَبِيْلَ	سَهِيْلَةَ
عِزِيْنَ	كُلِّ
أَخِى	فَرِيْقَانِ
صُحُفَ	عَشِيْرَتَكَ

Exercise
Word Search

مَ	ثَ	لُ	هُو	تَ	ظَ	هَ	رَا	رَا
عَ	مَ	لُ	هُو	هُو	مَ	هُو	تَ	ظَ
أُ	هُو	هُو	هُو	تَ	ظَ	عَ	رَا	سَ
هُو	تِي	وَ	رَ	سُ	و	لَ	هُو	أَ
هُو	ثُ	لَ	فُ	هُ	دِ	یَ	لَ	
مَ	ا	لُ	هُو	هُو	هُو	تَ	ظَ	كَ
هُو	تَ	ظَ	لَ	نُ	ذِ	ي	قُ	هُو
مَ	وَا	زِي	نُ	ه	هُو	تَ	ظَ	هُو

سَأَلَكَ	مَثَلُهُو
أَتَيْتُهُو	وَرَسُولَهُو
مَعَهُو	تَظْهَرَا
مَالُهُو	مَوَازِينه
لَنُذِيقُهُو	لَهُو
فَهَدَى	عَمَلُهُو

وَ	نُ	سُ	كِ	ى	دَ	ىَ	سَ	وَ
جَ	مَ	قِ	وِ	قَ	دَ	ىَ	بَ	ثَ
عَ	قَ	ىْ	ىْ	سَ	دَ	ىَ	ىْ	ا
لَ	ا	قُ	ضْ	ىَ	لِ	لِ	لِ	قَ
هُو	لِ	وَ	قِ	ىْ	لِ	هِء	ى	هُو
دَ	ىَ	سَ	سَدْ	فِ	لِ	ىْ	نَ	هِء
هِء	دَ	ىْ	سَ	دَ	ىْ	دَ	سَ	دَ
نَ	ىْ	ح	رِ	ف	مَ	ىْ	ظِ	عَ

عَظِيمَ	وَنُسُكِي
فَرِحِينَ	وَجَعَلَهُو
قِيلَ	وَثَاقَهُو
لَقُضِىَ	مَقَالِيدَ
قَوِىَ	سَبِيلِي
سَافِلِينَ	وَقِيلِهِء

107

SCAN ME

darulqurra.org

القاعدة السمنودية للمبتدئين

Chapter Four

Introduction to Ṣifāt ul Ḥurūf

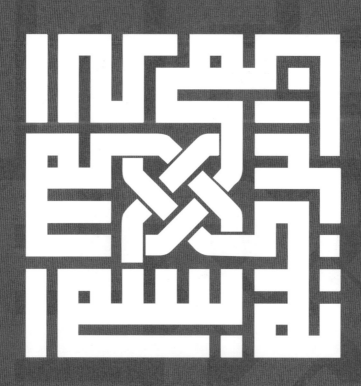

In this lesson, we will concentrate on the Sukūn symbol as well as some important characteristics of letters.

Sukūn symbols	أَيْ	أَيْ	أَيْ

Hams (continuation of breath)
& Rikhwah (continuation of sound)

☞ Express the characteristics in these letters by allowing the *sound* and *air* to flow without any interuptions or restrictions.

س	ص	خ	ش	ه	ث	ح	ف

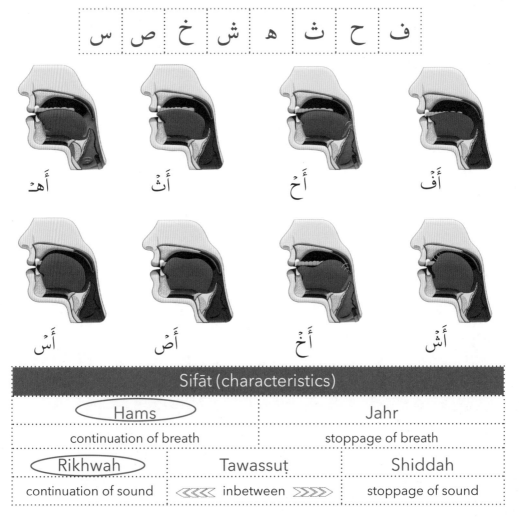

أَهْ	أَثْ	أَحْ	أَفْ

أَسْ	أَصْ	أَخْ	أَشْ

Sifāt (characteristics)		
Hams		Jahr
continuation of breath		stoppage of breath
Rikhwah	Tawassut	Shiddah
continuation of sound	⋘ inbetween ⋙	stoppage of sound

أَفْ	أَحْ	أَثْ	أَهـْ	أَشْ	أَخْ	أَصْ	أَسْ
إِفْ	إِحْ	إِثْ	إِهـْ	إِشْ	إِخْ	إِصْ	إِسْ
أُفْ	أُحْ	أُثْ	أُهـْ	أُشْ	أُخْ	أُصْ	أُسْ

Revision 4.1

Remember to continue reciting without spelling and differentiating the sound between the full and empty mouth, short and long letters clearly.

أَفْ	إِفْ	أُفْ	أَحْ	أَحْ	إِحْ	أُحْ	أَثْ	إِثْ
أُثْ	أَهـْ	إِهـْ	أُهـْ	أَشْ	إِشْ	أُشْ	أَخْ
إِخْ	أُخْ	أَصْ	إِصْ	أُصْ	أَسْ	إِسْ	أُسْ
أَحْ	إِحْ	أَفْ	إِفْ	أُهـْ	إِحْ	أُصْ	أَخْ
إِصْ	أَثْ	أُسْ	إِصْ	أُهـْ	أُخْ	إِهـْ	أُفْ
أُحْ	أُصْ	أُخْ	إِخْ	أَصْ	أَشْ	أُهـْ	إِحْ
أَحْ	إِصْ	إِشْ	أُفْ	إِهـْ	أُصْ	أَهـْ	أُشْ

Exercise

True/False

Circle either true or false if the statement is true or false.

Statements		
Makhraj and Sifāt are the same thing	True	(False)
Makhraj is were the letter is read from	True	False
Makhraj of a letter can change	True	False
Every letter has more than one Makhraj	True	False
Every letter has more than one Characteristic	True	False
Hams is the continuation of breath	True	False
Rikhwah is the continuation of breath	True	False
Rikhwah is the continuation of sound	True	False
Hams & Rikhwah are the same thing	True	False
8 letters have Hams & Rikhwah	True	False

Exercise

Note:

Hams (continuation of breath)
& Rikhwah (continuation of sound)

إِنْ	إِحْ	أُكَ	أُفَ	أُكَ	إِنْ	أَتْ	أُكَ	(إِصْ)
إِثْ	أَضْ	إِنْ	إِهـ	إِثْ	إِىْ	إِنْ	أَتْ	إِفْ
إِنْ	إِنْ	إِضْ	أُكَ	إِلْ	إِشْ	إِشْ	ئُوُ	إِضْ
أُكَ	أَتْ	إِىْ	أُزْ	أُحْ	أُهـ	إِلْ	أُفَ	إِىْ
أُحْ	إِنْ	إِلْ	أُسْ	أَثْ	أَتْ	أَتْ	أُصْ	أَتْ
إِنْ	أَضْ	أَغْ	إِنْ	أُكَ	أَتْ	أَظْ	إِظْ	أَتْ
أُثْ	إِلْ	إِضْ	أُثْ	إِنْ	إِشْ	إِلْ	إِنْ	إِضْ
أَتْ	إِهـ	إِىْ	أُزْ	أُحْ	إِلْ	إِضْ	أَتْ	إِىْ

In this lesson, we will continue to concentrate on the characteristics of letters whilst joining letters together.

Jahr (stoppage of breath)
& Rikhwah (continuation of sound)

☞   In the following letters the *sound* will not be interupted like the *air* flow.

ا و ي ذ ز ظ غ ض

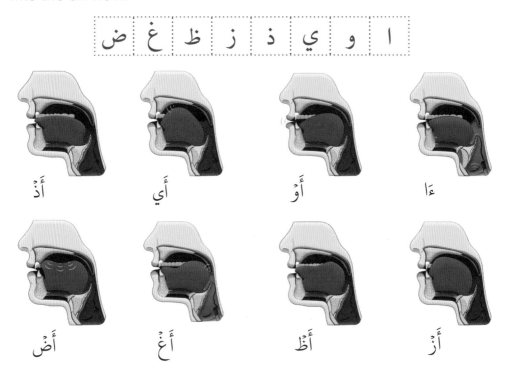

أَذْ   أَيْ   أَوْ   ءَا

أَضْ   أَغْ   أَظْ   أَزْ

Sifāt (characteristics)	
Hams	Jahr
continuation of breath	stoppage of breath

Rikhwah	Tawassuṭ	Shiddah
continuation of sound	≪≪≪ inbetween ≫≫≫	stoppage of sound

أَضْ	أَغْ	أَظْ	أَزْ	أَذْ	أَى	أُوْ	ءَا
أُذْ	أُوْ	إِظْ	إِضْ	إِغْ	إِظْ	إِزْ	إِذْ
		أُضْ	أُغْ	أُظْ	أُزْ		

Revision 4.2

Remember to continue reciting without spelling and differentiating the sound between the full and empty mouth, short and long letters clearly.

إِثْ	أَثْ	أُحْ	إِحْ	أَحْ	أُفْ	إِفْ	أَفْ
أَخْ	أُشْ	إِشْ	أَشْ	أُهْ	إِهْ	أَهْ	أُثْ
أُسْ	إِسْ	أَسْ	أُصْ	إِصْ	أَصْ	أُخْ	إِخْ
إِذْ	أَذْ	إِى	أَى	أُوْ	إِوْ	أُوْ	ءَا
أَغْ	أُظْ	إِظْ	أَظْ	أُزْ	إِزْ	أَزْ	أُذْ
أَسْ	أَزْ	أَفْ	أُوْ	أُضْ	إِضْ	أَضْ	إِغْ
إِثْ	أَضْ	أَغْ	إِهْ	إِثْ	إِى	أَظْ	إِظْ

Exercise
True/False

Circle either true or false if the statement is true or false.

Statements		
Makhaarij and Sifāt are two different things	(True)	False
Makhraj is were the letter is read from	True	False
Makhraj is the singular of Makhaarij	True	False
Jahr and Hams are the same but have different names	True	False
Every letter has Hams in it	True	False
Jahr is the stoppage of breath	True	False
Rikhwah is the continuation of breath	True	False
Rikhwah is the stoppage of sound	True	False
Jahr & Rikhwah are always together	True	False
8 letters have Jahr & Rikhwah also	True	False

Exercise
Word Search

Circle all the letters that contain the characteristics of Jahr &
Rikhwah in the table below.

Note:

Jahr (stoppage of breath)
& Rikhwah (continuation of sound)

أُزْ	إِحْ	إِضْ	أُفْ	أُكْ	ءَا	أَتْ	أُكْ	أَزْ
إِثْ	أَضْ	إِنْ	إِهْـ	إِثْ	أَزْ	إِنْ	أَتْ	إِفْ
أَغْ	أُظْ	إِظْ	إِثْ	أُزْ	إِزْ	أَزْ	أُذْ	إِضْ
أَسْ	أَزْ	أَفْ	أُوْ	أُضْ	إِشْ	أَضْ	إِغْ	إِىْ
إِثْ	أَضْ	أَظْ	إِهْـ	إِثْ	إِىْ	أَظْ	إِظْ	أَتْ
أُثْ	إِسْ	إِضْ	أُثْ	ءَا	إِشْ	إِشْ	ئُوْ	أَتْ
أُفْ	إِهْـ	إِىْ	أُزْ	أُحْ	أُهْـ	إِضْ	أُفْ	إِضْ
أُحْ	إِصْ	أَضْ	أَذْ	أُثْ	أَفْ	إِسْ	إِحْ	إِىْ

In this lesson, we will concentrate on the some important characteristics of letters whilst joining letters together.

Hams (continuation of breath)
& Shiddah (stoppage of sound)

☞   In the following two letters a small amount of breath/air is released after the sound has come to an end.

ك ت

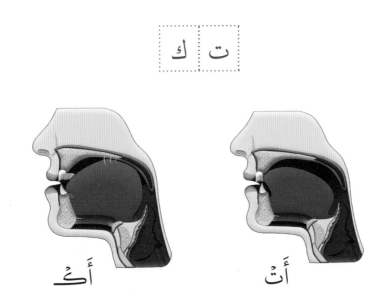

أَكُ   أَتُ

Sifāt (characteristics)		
Hams		Jahr
continuation of breath		stoppage of breath
Rikhwah	Tawassuṭ	Shiddah
continuation of sound	≪≪≪≪ inbetween ≫≫≫	stoppage of sound

أُكَ	إِكِ	أَكَ	أُتَ	إِتْ	أَتْ
لَكَ	قُضِيَتْ	تَتْبَعُهَا	أَكْرَمُ	فَعَدَلَكَ	فُتِحَتْ
فَتَحَتْ	ظَلَمَكَ	هَلَكَ	نُصِبَتْ	أَكْثَرُ	ضُرِبَتْ

Revision 4.3 📖

Remember to continue reciting without spelling and differentiating the sound between the full and empty mouth, short and long letters clearly.

خُلِقَتْ	نَجَحَتْ	فَتَحَتْ	نَصَرَتْ
فَطَرَتْ	فَتَحَلَكَ	نُصِبَتْ	رُفِعَتْ
أَتَاكَ	حَافِظْ	ظَهْرِهِ	مَسْرُورًا
حُشِرَتْ	يَحْيَىٰ	يَخْفَىٰ	سُطِحَتْ
هَزْلِ	أَظْلَمَ	نَضِجَتْ	إِهْدِنَا
ظُلِمَتْ	حَسَنَتْ	حُسْنَىٰ	أَشْقَىٰ
يَرْضَى	أَشْقَى	جُمِعَتْ	يَغْشَى
يَرْضَىٰ	أَعْلَىٰ	أَهْلَكْتُ	إِشْ

Exercise
True/False

Circle either true or false if the statement is true or false.

Statements		
Makhraj is were the letter is born from	(True)	False
Sifa is the singular of Sifāt	True	False
Makhaarij is the plural of Makhraj	True	False
Jahr is the stoppage of breath	True	False
Hams is the continuation of breath	True	False
Jahr is the opposite of Hams	True	False
Rikhwah is the opposite of Shiddah	True	False
Shiddah is the stoppage of sound	True	False
8 letters have Hams & Shiddah	True	False
Small amount of air is released after reading ت & ك	True	False

Exercise
Word Search

Circle all the letters that contain the characteristics of Hams &
Shiddah in the table below.

Note:

Hams (continuation of breath)
& Shiddah (stoppage of sound)

أُزْ	إِحْ	إِضْ	إِفْ	أُفَ	أُكْ	ءَا	أَتْ	أُكْ	أَتْ
إِثْ	أَضْ	إِنْ	إِهـْ	إِثْ	أَزْ	إِنْ	أَتْ	إِفَ
أَغْ	أُظْ	إِظْ	أَكْ	أُزْ	إِزْ	أَزْ	أُذْ	إِضْ
أَسْ	أَزْ	أَفَ	أُوْ	أُضْ	إِشْ	أَضْ	إِغْ	أُكْ
أَكْ	أَضْ	أَظْ	إِهـْ	إِثْ	إِىْ	أَظْ	أَكْ	أَتْ
أُثْ	إِسْ	إِضْ	أُثْ	ءَا	إِشْ	إِشْ	ئُوْ	أَتْ
أَفَ	أَكْ	إِىْ	أَكْ	أُحْ	أُهـْ	إِضْ	أَكْ	إِضْ
أُحْ	إِصْ	أَكْ	أَذْ	أُثْ	أَفَ	إِسْ	إِحْ	إِىْ

121

In this lesson, we will concentrate on important characteristics of letters whilst joining letters together.

Jahr (stoppage of breath)
& Tawassuṭ (not a complete stoppage or continuation of sound - inbetween Shiddah and Rikhwah)

👉   In the following letters the breath will stop whilst the sound will continue.

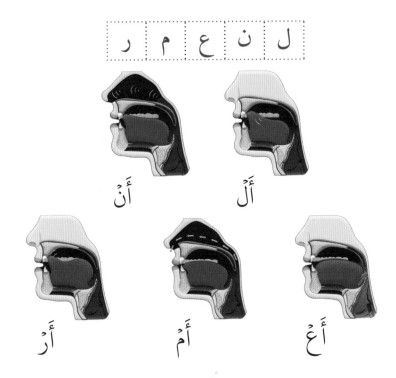

ر	م	ع	ن	ل

Sifāt (characteristics)		
Hams	Jahr	
continuation of breath	stoppage of breath	
Rikhwah	Tawassuṭ	Shiddah
continuation of sound	⫷⫷ inbetween ⫸⫸	stoppage of sound

أُنْ	إِنْ	أَنْ	أَلُ	إِلْ	أَلْ
أُمْ	إِمْ	أَمْ	أُعْ	إِعْ	أَعْ
أُرُ		إِرْ		أَرُ	

Revision 4.4

Remember to continue reciting without spelling and differentiating the sound between the full and empty mouth, short and long letters clearly.

مِنْ	لَمْ	أَرْضَ	أَمْهِلْهُمْ
نَعْبُدُ	مَنْ	صُلْبِ	فَلْيَنْظُرْ
ذٰلِكَ	عَلَيْكُمْ	أُرْسِلُوا	عَنْهَا
حُشِرَتْ	أَعْمَى	عَسْعَسَ	يَنْظُرُونَ
عِنْدَ	قُتِلَ الْإِنْسَانُ		إِهْدِنَا
فَأَنْتَ عَنْهُ	وَمَا صَاحِبُكُمْ		
خَلَقَ	وَهُوَ يَغْشَى		يَغْشَى
عَرْشٍ	ذٰلِكَ فَلْيَتَنَا		أُزْلِفَتْ

Exercise
True/False

Circle either true or false if the statement is true or false.

Statements		
Hams is the continuation of breath	(True)	False
Rikhwah is the continuation of breath	True	False
Rikhwah is the continuation of sound	True	False
Hams & Rikhwah are the same thing	True	False
8 letters have Hams & Rikhwah	True	False
Tawassuṭ is the opposite of Shiddah	True	False
Shiddah is the stoppage of sound	True	False
Tawassuṭ sits between Shiddah & Rikhwah	True	False
Jahr is the stoppage of breath	True	False
5 letters have Jahr & Tawassuṭ	True	False

Exercise
Word Search

Circle all the letters that contain the characteristics of Jahr &
Tawassuṭ in the table below.

Note:

Jahr (stoppage of breath)
& Tawassuṭ (not a complete stoppage or continuation of sound
- inbetween Shiddah and Rikhwah)

أُزْ	إِرْ	إِضْ	أَعْ	أُمْ	إِرْ	إِلْ	أَكْ	أَعْ
إِثْ	أَضْ	إِنْ	إِهـْ	أُمْ	أُزْ	إِنْ	أَتْ	إِلْ
أَعْ	أُظْ	أَنْ	أَكْ	أُزْ	إِزْ	أَزْ	أُذْ	إِضْ
أُمْ	أَزْ	أَفْ	أُمْ	أَعْ	إِرْ	إِلْ	إِغْ	أَكْ
أَكْ	إِلْ	أَظْ	إِهـْ	إِثْ	إِىْ	أَظْ	أَكْ	أَتْ
أَنْ	إِسْ	إِضْ	أُثْ	إِرْ	أُمْ	إِشْ	ئُوْ	أَنْ
أُفْ	أَكْ	إِىْ	أَكْ	أُحْ	أُهـْ	إِضْ	أُمْ	إِضْ
إِرْ	إِصْ	أَعْ	أَذْ	أُثْ	أُمْ	إِسْ	أَنْ	إِىْ

In this lesson, we will concentrate on important characteristics of letters whilst joining letters together.

Jahr (stoppage of breath)
& Shiddah (stoppage of sound)

☛   In the following letters the air and sound are forced to stop completely. The first five letters will be recited with a Qalqalah in order to differentiate the sounds from one another.

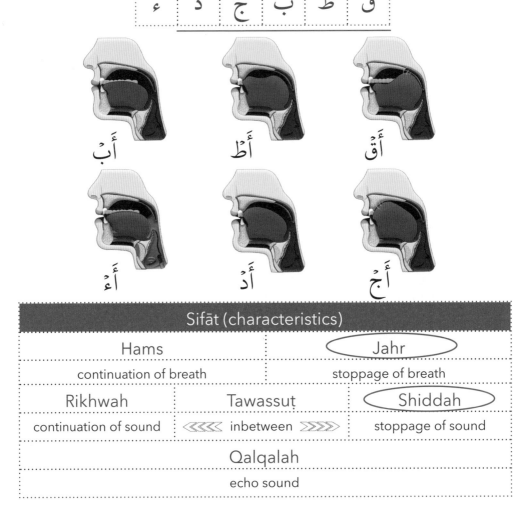

| ء | د | ج | ب | ط | ق |

Sifāt (characteristics)		
Hams		Jahr
continuation of breath		stoppage of breath
Rikhwah	Tawassuṭ	Shiddah
continuation of sound	⟪⟪⟪ inbetween ⟫⟫⟫	stoppage of sound
Qalqalah		
echo sound		

أُطْ	إِطْ	أَطْ	أُقْ	إِق	أَقْ
أُجْ	إِجْ	أَجْ	أُبْ	إِب	أَبْ
أُءْ	إِءْ	أَءْ	أُدْ	إِد	أَدْ

Revision 4.5

Remember to continue reciting without spelling and differentiating the sound between the full and empty mouth, short and long letters clearly.

أَطْعَمَهُمْ	لَمْ يَلِدْ وَلَمْ يُولَدْ	فَلَقْ
نَعْبُدْ	أَدْرَاكَ	طَبَقْ	هُوَ الْأَبْتَرُ
لَمْ يُخْلَقْ	سَنُقْرِئُكَ	وَالْفَجْرِ	تُبْلَى
إِقْرَأْ	وَسَقْيَهَا	وَجْهِ	وَادْخُلِى
رَدَدْنَهُ	أَلَمْ نَجْعَلِ الْأَرْضَ مَهْدًا	إِهْدِنَا
أَلَمْ نَشْرَحْ لَكَ صَدْرَكَ	أَلَمْ يَجِدْكَ
قَدَرِ	وَخَلَقْنَكُمْ	لَيَطْغَى
جِئْنَا	لَقَدْ خَلَقْنَا الْإِنْسَانَ	تَجْرِىْ

Exercise
True/False

Circle either true or false if the statement is true or false.

Statements		
Hams is the continuation of breath	(True)	False
Rikhwah is the continuation of sound	True	False
Tawassuṭ means inbetween Rikhwah & Hams	True	False
Tawassuṭ means inbetween Rikhwah & Shiddah	True	False
5 letters have Jahr & Tawassuṭ	True	False
5 letters have Qalqalah	True	False
Qalqalah is the opposite of Jahr	True	False
Tawassuṭ sits between Shiddah & Rikhwah	True	False
Jahr is the opposite of Hams	True	False
Rikhwah is the opposite of Shiddah	True	False

Exercise
Word Search

Circle all the letters that contain the characteristics of Jahr &
Tawassuṭ in the table below.

Note:

Jahr (stoppage of breath)
& Tawassuṭ (not a complete stoppage or continuation of sound
- inbetween Shiddah and Rikhwah)

أُزْ	إِقْ	أُبْ	أَعْ	إِبْ	أُبْ	إِءْ	أُلْكْ	أَقْ
إِثْ	أَضْ	إِنْ	إِدْ	أُمْ	أَزْ	أُدْ	أَتْ	إِلْ
أَءْ	إِءْ	أُجْ	أَكْ	أُزْ	أَقْ	أَزْ	أُذْ	إِءْ
أُدْ	أَزْ	أَفْ	أَمْ	أَعْ	إِدْ	إِلْ	أُجْ	أُبْ
أَكْ	أُبْ	أَءْ	أُجْ	إِثْ	أُبْ	أُجْ	أَكْ	أَتْ
إِقْ	أَقْ	إِضْ	أُثْ	إِرْ	أُمْ	إِشْ	إِءْ	إِقْ
أَفْ	أَكْ	إِىْ	أُبْ	إِبْ	أَقْ	إِضْ	أُدْ	إِضْ
أُدْ	إِصْ	أُدْ	أَذْ	أُثْ	أُمْ	إِبْ	أَنْ	أَءْ

In this lesson, we will concentrate on important characteristics of letters whilst joining letters together.

Letters of Leen (delicate & ease)

👉 The following two letters are pronounced with great ease and are known as the letters of *Leen.*

ي	و

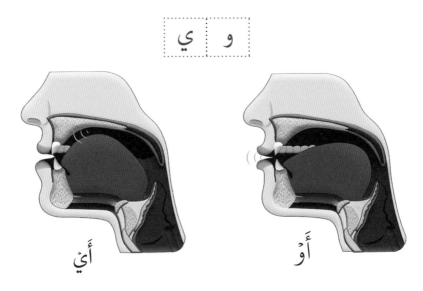

أَيْ   أَوْ

Sifāt (characteristics)		
Hams		Jahr
continuation of breath		stoppage of breath
Rikhwah	Tawassuṭ	Shiddah
continuation of sound	⋘ inbetween ⋙	stoppage of sound
Qalqalah		
echo sound		
Leen		
delicate & ease		

تَىْ	تَوْ	بَىْ	بَوْ	أَىْ	أَوْ
قَىْ	قَوْ	فَىْ	فَوْ	سَىْ	سَوْ
كَىْ	كَوْ	طَىْ	طَوْ	رَىْ	رَوْ

Revision 4.6

Remember to continue reciting without spelling and differentiating the sound between the full and empty mouth, short and long letters clearly.

غَيْب	مَوْتُ	سَوْفَ	حَوْلَ
لَيْسَ	قَوْمُ	أَوْحَيْنَا	بَيْنَ
وَيْلُ	قَوْمُ	لَارَيْبَ	خَيْرِ
عَلَيْهِم	صَيْفِ	أَرَئَيْتَ	بَيْتِ
يَوْمَ	أَلَمْ تَرَكَيْفَ فَعَلَ		عَيْنَ
أَوْضُحْهَا	وَهَدَيْنَهُ	وَلَسَوْفَ	عَلَيْنَا
لَقَوْلُ	يَوْمَ يَنْظُرُ	لَيْلَ	يَرَوْنَهَا
كَيْفَ سُطِحَتْ	مَوْعُودِ	وَإِذَا رَأَوْهُمْ	بِأَيْدِى

Exercise
True/False

Circle either true or false if the statement is true or false.

Statements		
Makhraj is were the letter is born from	(True)	False
Sifa is the singular of Sifāt	True	False
Makhaarij is the plural of Makhraj	True	False
Leen letters are read with delicate & ease	True	False
Jahr is the opposite of Hams	True	False
Rikhwah is the opposite of Shiddah	True	False
Leen also has 8 letters in total	True	False
Tawassuṭ is the opposite of Shiddah	True	False
Shiddah is the stoppage of sound	True	False
5 letters have Qalqalah	True	False

Exercise
Word Search

Circle all the letters that contain the characteristics of Jahr &
Tawassuṭ in the table below.

Note:

Jahr (stoppage of breath)
& Tawassuṭ (not a complete stoppage or continuation of sound
- inbetween Shiddah and Rikhwah)

أُرْ	إِقْ	أُبْ	أَعْ	طَو	أَوْ	إِءْ	أَكْ	أَوْ
طَو	أَضْ	إِنْ	إِدْ	أُمْ	أَزْ	أُدْ	أَتْ	بَىْ
أَىْ	بَىْ	أُجْ	أَوْ	أُزْ	أَقْ	أَزْ	أُذْ	إِءْ
أُدْ	أَزْ	أَىْ	أُمْ	أَعْ	تَىْ	طَو	أَىْ	أُبْ
أَكْ	تَىْ	أَءْ	طَو	بَىْ	أُبْ	أَوْ	أَكْ	أَتْ
بَىْ	أَقْ	أَوْ	أُثْ	إِرْ	أُمْ	بَىْ	طَو	إِقْ
أُفْ	أَكْ	إِىْ	أُبْ	إِبْ	أَقْ	أَوْ	أُدْ	إِضْ
أُدْ	أَىْ	أُدْ	أَذْ	أُثْ	أُمْ	إِبْ	أَنْ	أَءْ

In this lesson we will concentrate on important characteristics of letters whilst joining letters together.

Letters of Safīr (buzzing or whistling sound)

☞ The following three letters are pronounced with a buzzing or a whistle sound.

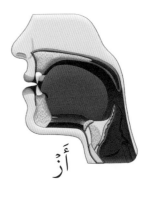 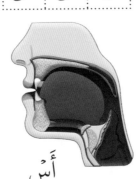 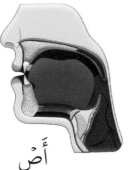

Summary of Sifāt (characteristics)		
Hams		Jahr
continuation of breath		stoppage of breath
Rikhwah	Tawassut	Shiddah
continuation of sound	⋘ inbetween ⋙	stoppage of sound
Qalqalah		
echo sound		
Leen		
delicate & ease		
Safīr		
buzzing or whistling sound		
Tafkhīm		
full mouth sound (see page 46)		

أَزْ	أَصْ	أَسْ	أَصْ	أَسْ	أَزْ
إِزْ	إِصْ	إِسْ	إِصْ	إِسْ	إِزْ
أُزْ	أُسْ	أُصْ	أُزْ	أُسْ	أُصْ

Revision 4.7

Remember to continue reciting without spelling and differentiating the sound between the full and empty mouth, short and long letters clearly.

سَوْط	إِذَا عَسْعَسَ	سَوْفَ	أَسْفَلَ
لَا يَصِلُهَا	يَسْفِكُ	فَبَصُرَت	لَيْسَ
زَيْتُونَ	أُزْلِفَت	فَصْلٌ	نُصِبَت
بِالْحُسْنَى	مُعْصِرَاتٍ	فَصِيلَتِهِ ۦ	وَصَاحِبَتِهِ ۦ

Exercise
True/False

Circle either true or false if the statement is true or false.

Statements		
Hams is the continuation of sound	True	(False)
Rikhwah is the stoppage of breath	True	False
Rikhwah is the continuation of breath	True	False
Qalqalah letters are د ـ ج ـ ب ـ ط ـ ق	True	False
Qalqalah letters are ء ـ د ـ ج ـ ب ـ ط ـ ق	True	False
Hams is the opposite of Shiddah	True	False
Shiddah is the stoppage of sound & breath	True	False
Tawassuṭ sits between Hams & Jahr	True	False
Safīr is the stoppage of breath	True	False
Safīr has 3 letters	True	False

Statements		
Safir letters have a buzzing or whistling sound	True	False
Leen letters are read with delicate & ease	True	False
Leen has 2 letters	True	False
Leen, Qalqalah and Safir dont have opposites	True	False
Sifa is the plural of Sifāt	True	False

Exercise
Word Search

ثُ	بَ	صِ	نُ	سَ	أَ	لُ	صُ	أَ
زَ	بِ	فَ	سَ	لُ	صُ	فَ	عَ	يَ
ئ	ا	تُ	فَ	لِ	زُ	أُ	ئَ	سَ
تُ	لُ	هِ	بُ	و	عُ	شُ	ا	فِ
وُ	حُ	ئ	لَ	فَ	سَ	أَ	لَ	كُ
نَ	سُ	دُ	طَ	وَ	سَ	مُ	مَ	دًا
نَ	نُ	تِ	تِ	ا	رَ	صِ	عُ	مُ
دِ	ى	ا	هـ	لُ	صُ	يَ	ا	لَ

أَسَ	أَصُ
نُصِبَتُ	فَضُلُ
أُزِلِفَتُ	زَيْتُوْنَ
لَايَصُلِهَا	مُعُصِرَاتٍ
بِالحُسْنٰى	يَسُفِكُ
سَوْطَ	أَسُفَلَ

Exercise
Word Search

يَ	صْ	أَ	يَ	شْ	لَ	فَ	سْ	أَ		
غْ	شْ	هْ	شْ	ئ	صْ	أَ	إِ	مَ	مَسْرُورَا	أَسْفَلَ
شْ	صْ	أَ	سَ	سَ	شْ	هْ	هْ	سْ	سُطِحَتْ	لَيْسَ
ى	شْ	هْ	شْ	قَ	دِ	شْ	شْ	رُ	إِهْدِنَا	نُصِبَتْ
ثْ	حَ	طِ	ئ	نَ	شْ	نُ	نُ	وْ	أَشْقَى	أَوْ
صْ	إِ	ا	ا	شْ	صْ	صْ	أَ	رَ	يَغْشَى	أَصْ
ا	شْ	إِ	لَ	بَ	شْ	هْ	ا		إِشْ	إِصْ
ثْ	حَ	طِ	ثْ	حَ	طِ	سُ	وْ	أَ		

كُ	فِ	سْ	يَ	ى	نْ	ا	ذَ	إِ		
مُ	زْ	إِ	ثْ	فَ	لِ	زْ	أُ	صْ	سَوْطَ	إِذَا
عْ	إِ	ثْ	فَ	لِ	زْ	نْ	ى	نْ	لَا	يَسْفِكُ
صِ	نْ	ى	نْ	إِ	فَ	ثْ	لِ	زْ	زَيْتُونَ	أُزْلِفَتْ
رَ	نْ	ى	نْ	سْ	حُ	لَ	ا	بْ	بِالْحُسْنَى	مُعْصِرَاتٍ
ا	زْ	أُ	إِ	ثْ	فَ	لِ	زْ	أُ	إِزْ	إِصْ
تِ	زَ	زْ	نَ	ى	ثُ	ئ	زَ	زْ		أُزْ
طَ	وْ	سَ	ى	نْ	سُ	أُ	ا	لَ		أُسْ

Exercise
Word Search

مَ	وُ	يَ	بَ	ئ	تِ	بَ	ئ	غَ
ا	عَ	يَ	أَئ	ا	نَ	ئ	لَ	عَ
لُ	ئ	وَ	بِ	عَ	أَئ	وَ	بَ	أَ
كَ	نَ	ئ	لَ	لَ	خَ	أَئ	لَ	وُ
ةُ	دِ	ئ	تِ	ئ	بَ	ئ	تِ	ضُ
ئ	هِ	أَئ	رِ	سَ	بَ	ئ	تِ	حَ
م	أَئ	ا	ا	هَ	حَ٘	ضُ	وُ	أَ
ا	تَ	ةِ	ا	هَ	نَ	وُ	رَ	يَ

غَيْب	خَيْرِ
لَيْسَ	بَيْتِ
وَيْلُ	عَيْن
عَلَيْهِم	عَلَيْنَا
يَوْمَ	يَرَوْنَهَا
بِأَيْدِئ	أَوْضَحْـهَا

هَ	أَئَي	رَ	أَ	فَ	تْ	قَ	لِ	خُ
زُ	تْ	رَ	شِ	حُ	هَ	أَئَي	رَ	لَا
لِ	لَا	تَ	أَئَي	أَ	فَ	وُ	سَ	لَا
أَئَي	رَ	لَا	ظُ	لَا	طَ	هَ	أَئَي	وَ
ثْ	رَ	لِ	لَا	لَا	رَ	إِ	لَا	لَا
لَا	مَ	لَ	ثْ	رَ	ذَ	لَا	لَا	لَا
ثْ	ئ	لَا	ئ	لَا	ا	كَ	تَ٘	أَ
لَ	لَا	بَ	ا	نَ	ئ	حَ	وَ	أَ

خُلِقَتْ	سَوْفَ
فَطَرَتْ	أوحَيْنَا
أَتَـكَ	لَارَيْبَ
حُشِرَتْ	أَرَئَيْتَ
هَزِلِ	لَيَلَ
ظُلِمَتْ	وَإِذَا

SCAN ME

darulqurra.org

القاعدة السمنودية للمبتدئين

Chapter Five

Shamsiyya & Qamariyya
Tanwīn, Sukūn, Tashdīd & Waqf

In this lesson, we will look at the letters of the throat.

- Read without spelling and differentiate the sounds between each letter.

- Remind the learners that the Alif that follows Faṭḥatayn is always silent unless Waqf (stop) is done. In that case we will drop one Faṭḥah and read the Alif as a Madd like in chapter three.

- Each letter should be repeated after the tutor, ensuring the learner differentiates between the two sounds. This can be achieved by a short pause between each letter.

الحروف الحلقية							
حَنْ	حَا	عَنْ	عَا	هَنْ	هًا	أَنْ	ءاً
حِنْ	حِ	عِنْ	عِ	هِنْ	ٍه	إِنْ	ءٍ
حُنْ	حُ	عُنْ	عُ	هُنْ	ٌه	أُنْ	ءٌ

الحروف اللهوية				الحروف الحلقية			
كَنْ	گَا	قَنْ	قَّ	خَنْ	خَا	غَنْ	غَا
كِنْ	گِ	قِنْ	قِ	خِنْ	خِ	غِنْ	غِ
كُنْ	گُ	قُنْ	قُ	خُنْ	خُ	غُنْ	غُ

الحروف الشجرية							
شَا	شَنْ	جَا	جَنْ	يَا	يَنْ	ضَا	ضَنْ
شِ	شِنْ	جِ	جِنْ	ىِ	يِنْ	ضِ	ضِنْ
شُ	شُنْ	جُّ	جُنْ	ئُ	يُنْ	ضُ	ضُنْ

الحروف النطعية		الحروف الذلقية					
دَا	دَنْ	رَا	رَنْ	نَا	نَنْ	لَا	لَنْ
دِ	دِنْ	رِ	رِنْ	نِ	نِنْ	لِ	لِنْ
دُ	دُنْ	رُ	رُنْ	نُ	نُنْ	لُ	لُنْ

الحروف الأسلية				الحروف النطعية			
صَا	صَنْ	سَا	سَنْ	طَا	طَنْ	تَا	تَنْ
صِ	صِنْ	سِ	سِنْ	طِ	طِنْ	تِ	تِنْ
صُ	صُنْ	سُ	سُنْ	طُ	طُنْ	تُ	تُنْ

الحروف اللثوية						الحروف الأسلية	
ظَ	ظَنْ	ثَا	ثَنْ	ذَا	ذَنْ	زَا	زَنْ
ظِ	ظِنْ	ثِ	ثِنْ	ذِ	ذِنْ	زِ	زِنْ
ظُ	ظُنْ	ثُ	ثُنْ	ذُ	ذُنْ	زُ	زُنْ

الحروف الشفوية							
وَنْ	وَا	بَنْ	بَا	مَنْ	مَّا	فَنْ	فَا
وِنْ	وِ	بِنْ	بِ	مِنْ	مِ	فِنْ	فٍ
وُنْ	وُ	بُنْ	بُ	مُنْ	مُّ	فُنْ	فُ

Exercise
Word Search

وَ	يْ	لُ	عِ	يْ	نَ	قَ	ا	شَ
خَ	عَ	ظِ	يْ	مٍ	سَ	فَ	عَ	فَ
بِ	يَ	مٍ	يْ	جَ	مٍ	يْ	عًا	عَ
أ	ا	شُ	عُ	و	بُ	هِ	لِ	ةٌ
حَ	لَ	هَ	بِ	ةَ	لِ	يْ	صُ	ظِ
دَا	مَ	مُ	نَ	ا	يْ	دُ	نْ	يْ
أ	بِ	يْ	رِ	نْ	نَ	تِ	ذُ	نْ
مٍ	يْ	زَ	ا	نِ	حَ	ا	سِ	دِ

وَيْل	ذُنْ
صُنْ	رِنْ
أَحَدًا	حَاسِدٍ
عَظِيمٍ	شَفَعَةٌ
لَهَبٍ	جَمِيعًا
مِيزَانٍ	شُعُوبٌ

Revision 5.1

Remember to continue reciting without spelling and differentiating the sound between the full and empty mouth, short and long letters clearly.

ءَا	عَا	جِ	رِ	گَا	قَا
ظِ	طِ	سُ	صُ	صِ	يِ
ءِ	جِ	ذِ	زِ	ةُ	حُ
حِ	هِ	ةُ	تِ	غُ	خُ
كِ	قِ	صُ	سُ	حُ	عُ
قِ	هَا	رُ	رِ	رَ	لُ
كِ	ءِ	عُ	ءَا	ءِ	حَا
ضِ	دِ	ضُ	دُ	ضَ	دَ
صُ	سُ	صِ	يِ	صَ	سَ
عَا	ءَا	عِ	ءِ	عُ	ءُ

In this lesson, we will be looking at Shaddah (sign of emphasis) also known as Tashdīd.

حَقّ	حَقْ + قْ	إِنَّ	إِنْ + نَ
هَشّ	هَشْ + شْ	يُمِلَّ	يُمِلْ + لَ
رَبَّ	رَبْ + بَ	تَرَبُّص	تَرَبْ + بُصْ
عَمّ	عَمْ + مَ	صَبَّارٍ	صَبْ + بَارٍ

يَكُفَّ	عِزُّ	فَرَّ	فَأَمُّهُ	مِتُّ
يَحِلُّ	يَلُفُّ	صَبَّ	صَدُّوكُمْ	لَفَّ
فَوَلِّ	يَفِرُّ	يَخْتَصُّ	غُدُوُّهَا	زَقُّومٍ
تُبَّع	يَصُبُّ	يُؤَلِّف	يُكَوِّرُ	يُبَدَّلُ
وَسَبِّحْهُ	تَبَيَضُّ	كَطَيِّ	تُبَوِّئُ	عِلِّيُّونَ
مَتَّعْنَا	كُلُّهُنَّ	عِصِيُّهُمْ	يَسَّمَّعُونَ	يُسَيِّرُكُمْ

Revision 5.2 📖

Remember to continue reciting without spelling and differentiating the sound between the full and empty mouth, short and long letters clearly.

خُشُبٌ	كَادِحٌ	ضَلَـٰلًا	لَهَبٍ	أَلِيمًا
عَابِدٌ	شَاكِرٌ	طَهُورٌ	رَغَدًا	غَضَبٌ
كَرِيمًا	أُمَمٌ	حَسَنًا	حَاسِدٍ	جَمِيعًا
شُوَاظٌ	قَرْيَةٍ	هُدًى	صَعِيدًا	غَاسِقٍ
حَرَجٌ	صَبْرًا	طَعَامًا	كَرِيمًا	حَكِيمًا
رَبْوَةٍ	خَافِيَةٌ	مِيزَانٍ	ضَلَلٍ	قَلَمٌ
لَبَلَغًا	حِجَابٍ	أَحَدًا	سَابِقٌ	قُعُودًا
فُرَاتٌ	مِلْحٌ	مُبَـٰرَكًا	عَلِيمًا	شُعُوبٌ
شَيْخٌ	رِجَالٌ	شَفَعَةٌ	ظُلُمَتٍ	عَظِيمٍ
عَاصِفٌ	ثَابِتٌ	عَذَابٍ	رَيْحٌ	سَمِيعًا
وَمَعِينٍ	وَاسِعٌ	فَإِذَا هُوَ زَاهِقٌ		زَاهِقٌ
بَرْزَخٌ إِلَىٰ يَوْمِ يُبْعَثُونَ		وَلِبَاسُهُمْ فِيهَا حَرِيرٌ		خَالِصَةٌ

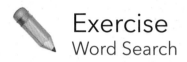

Exercise
Word Search

تُ	ا	قَ	مَ	كُ	رُ	يِّ	سَ	يُ
بَّ	عَ	فَ	هُ	مُّ	أُ	فَ	ب	خَ
عِ	ا	كِ	صَ	مَ	كُ	و	دُ	صَ
يِّ	طَ	كَ	بَّ	هُ	حْ	بِّ	سَ	وَ
ظِ	مِ	يِ	ا	ةَ	لَ	يِ	هِ	سَ
يِ	يِ	نَ	رِ	ا	فُ	لِّ	أَؤ	يُ
مَّ	عَ	تِ	ا	نَ	عْ	تَّ	مَ	أَ
رُ	وِّ	كَ	يُ	يِ	نَّ	هُ	لُّ	كُ

يُكَوِّرُ	كَظِّ	صَدُّوكُمْ	تُبَع	فَأُمُّهُ	يُسَيِّرُكُمْ
يُؤَلِّفُ	عَمَّ	صَبَّارٍ	مَتَّعْنَا	كُلُّهُنَّ	وَسَبِّحْهُ

Revision 5.3

Remember to continue reciting without spelling and differentiating the sound between the full and empty mouth, short and long letters clearly.

مَكْظُومٌ أُوفِدَ	وَمَتَاعٌ إِلَى حِينٍ	لَهُمْ فِيهَا زَفِيرٌ
ذُو فَضْلٍ عَظِيمٍ	فِيهَا فَوَاكِهُ كَثِيرَةٌ	غِلْظَةً أُوتِينَا
حَدِيثًا طَبَقًا	نَبَأَهُ بَعْدَ حِينٍ	يُرْسَلُ عَلَيْكُمَا شُوَاظٌ
قَالَ لَهُ صَاحِبُهُ	لَا يَجِدُونَ نِكَاحًا	كَثِيرَةٌ وِرْدًا
طَعَامٌ ظَلِيلٍ	تِجَارَةً حَاضِرَةً	هَذَا شَيْءٌ عَجِيبٌ
وَأُخَرَ يَبِسَاتٍ	هُنَالِكَ ثُبُورًا	لَقَادِرٌ رِيبَةً
خَشَبٌ عَلَقَةٍ	بِسَلَمٍ ءَامِنِينَ	خَاوِيَةٌ عَلَى عُرُوشِهَا
يَهْدِى بِهِ كَثِيرًا	وَمَتَاعٌ إِلَى حِينٍ	كُوبٍ سُورٍ
مَيْدَانٌ عَظِيمٍ	فِي مَقَامٍ أَمِينٍ	يَكُونُ لِي غُلَامٌ
ذِى ثَلَاثِ شُعَبٍ	قَالَ هَذِهِ نَاقَةٌ	وَلَيَالٍ عَشْرٍ

Note that the Lām Shamsiyyah is a silent letter marked in grey with a Hamzatul Waṣl before it. It is normally written as an empty Alif or more commonly with an Alif with a small unique symbol (ٱ) above it.

- Hamzatul Waṣl is an extra Hamzah that is written and recited in the begining of a word but dropped when joining a letter or word before it.

قُلْ أَعُوذُ بِرَبِّ ٱلنَّاسِ   ٱلنَّاس

Hamzah here is written   Hamzah here is written
but not recited   and recited

- Hamzatul Waṣl should not be mistaken for an Alif, which is always silent but rather recited clearly as a Hamzah (أ) when found at the begining of a word.

ٱلصَّعِقَةُ	ٱلصَّعِقَةُ	ٱلطَّارِقِ	ٱلطَّارِقِ
ٱلـذُّبَابُ	ٱلذُّبَابُ	ٱلتَّقْوَىٰ	ٱلتَّقْوَىٰ
ٱلضَّأْنِ	ٱلضَّأْنِ	ٱلرَّأْسُ	ٱلرَّأْسُ
ٱلسَّـٰجِدُونَ	ٱلسَّـٰجِدُونَ	ٱلثَّوَابُ	ٱلثَّوَابُ
ٱلصَّرْحَ	ٱلصَّرْحَ	ٱلتَّرَاقِ	ٱلتَّرَاقِ
ٱلصُّدُورِ	ٱلصُّدُورِ	ٱلرَّحِيمُ	ٱلرَّحِيمُ
ٱلـدِّينِ	ٱلدِّينِ	ٱلسَّحَرَةَ	ٱلسَّحَرَةَ
ٱلـثَّقَلَانِ	ٱلثَّقَلَانِ	ٱلظَّالِمِينَ	ٱلظَّالِمِينَ

Revision 5.4

Remember to continue reciting without spelling and differentiating the sound between the full and empty mouth, short and long letters clearly.

ٱلصَّٰعِقَةُ	ٱلثَّوَابُ	ٱلطَّارِقِ
ٱلذُّبَابُ	ٱلتَّرَاقِيَ	ٱلتَّقْوَىٰ
ٱلضَّأْنِ	ٱلصَّرْحَ	ٱلرَّأْسُ
ٱلثَّقَلَانِ	ٱلسَّٰجِدُونَ	ٱلظَّٰلِمِينَ

يُولِجُ ٱللَّيْلَ فِى ٱلنَّهَارِ
هُوَ ٱلتَّوَّابُ ٱلرَّحِيمُ
ٱلشَّهْرُ ٱلْحَرَامُ بِٱلشَّهْرِ ٱلْحَرَامِ
لَعَلَّنَا نَتَّبِعُ ٱلسَّحَرَةَ

أَرَءَيْتَ ٱلَّذِى يُكَذِّبُ بِٱلدِّينِ	قُلْ أَعُوذُ بِرَبِّ ٱلنَّاسِ
وَ تَوَاصَوْاْ بِٱلصَّبْرِ	مَلِكِ ٱلنَّاسِ
أَلْهَىٰكُمُ ٱلتَّكَاثُرُ	إِلَٰهِ ٱلنَّاسِ
وَ حُصِّلَ مَا فِى ٱلصُّدُورِ	قُلْ هُوَ ٱللَّهُ أَحَدٌ
فَمَا يُكَذِّبُكَ بَعْدُ بِٱلدِّينِ	ٱللَّهُ ٱلصَّمَدُ

In this lesson, we will be looking at the Lām Qamariyyah, which is opposite to the Lām Shamsiyyah and is always recited. Lām Qamariyyah also has a Hamzatul Waṣl (اَ) before it like the Lām Shamsiyyah.

اَلْيَتِيمِ	اَلْيَتِيمِ	اَلْإِسْلٰمِ	اَلْإِسْلٰمِ
بِالْحَقِّ	بِالْحَقِّ	اَلْحَمْدُ	اَلْحَمْدُ
اَلْبَيْتِ	اَلْبَيْتِ	اَلْقَمَرُ	اَلْقَمَرُ
اَلْوَسْوَاسِ	اَلْوَسْوَاسِ	اَلْمَاعُونَ	اَلْمَاعُونَ
اَلْبَيْتِ	اَلْبَيْتِ	اَلْأَرْضُ	اَلْأَرْضُ
اَلْخَنَّاسِ	اَلْخَنَّاسِ	اَلْجَنَّةِ	اَلْجَنَّةِ
اَلْكٰفِرُونَ	اَلْكٰفِرُونَ	اَلْعٰلَمِينَ	اَلْعٰلَمِينَ
اَلْوَسْوَاسِ	اَلْوَسْوَاسِ	اَلْفَلَقِ	اَلْفَلَقِ

فَلْيَعْبُدُوا رَبَّ هٰذَا الْبَيْتِ	حَمَّالَةَ الْحَطَبِ
أَلَمْ تَرَ كَيْفَ فَعَلَ رَبُّكَ بِأَصْحٰبِ الْفِيلِ	إِنَّ الْإِنْسَانَ لَفِى خُسْرٍ
وَ تَوَاصَوْا بِالْحَقِّ	فَذٰلِكَ الَّذِى يَدُعُّ الْيَتِيمَ
حَتّٰى زُرْتُمُ الْمَقَابِرَ	وَ لَا يَحُضُّ عَلٰى طَعَامِ الْمِسْكِينِ
كَلَّا لَوْ تَعْلَمُونَ عِلْمَ الْيَقِينِ	وَ يَمْنَعُونَ الْمَاعُونَ

Revision 5.5

Remember to continue reciting without spelling and differentiating the sound between the full and empty mouth, short and long letters clearly.

ٱلْبَيْتِ	ٱلْإِسْلَمِ	ٱلْمَاعُونَ	ٱلْفَلَقِ	ٱلْأَرْضُ
ٱلْخَنَّاسِ	ٱلْحَمْدُ	ٱلْوَسْوَاسِ	ٱلْقَمَرُ	ٱلْجِنَّةِ
ٱلْكَفِرُونَ	أَلَمْ تَرَ كَيْفَ فَعَلَ رَبُّكَ بِأَصْحَبِ ٱلْفِيلِ			ٱلْعَلَمِينَ
مِنَ ٱلْجِنَّةِ وَٱلنَّاسِ	حَمَّالَةَ ٱلْحَطَبِ		قُلْ أَعُوذُ بِرَبِّ ٱلْفَلَقِ	
وَتَوَاصَوْا بِٱلْحَقِّ		إِنَّ ٱلْإِنْسَانَ لَفِي خُسْرٍ		
وَلَا يَحُضُّ عَلَىٰ طَعَامِ ٱلْمِسْكِينِ		فَذَلِكَ ٱلَّذِى يَدُعُّ ٱلْيَتِيمَ		
فَلْيَعْبُدُوا رَبَّ هَذَا ٱلْبَيْتِ		وَيَمْنَعُونَ ٱلْمَاعُونَ		
كَلَّا لَوْ تَعْلَمُونَ عِلْمَ ٱلْيَقِينِ		حَتَّىٰ زُرْتُمُ ٱلْمَقَابِرَ		
وَمِنْ شَرِّ ٱلنَّفَّثَتِ فِي ٱلْعُقَدِ		مِنْ شَرِّ ٱلْوَسْوَاسِ ٱلْخَنَّاسِ		

In this lesson, we will be looking at Shaddah (sign of emphasis) with Tanwīn.

Tashdīd with Tanwīn			
Practice			
طِبٍّ	طِبٌّ	طِبَّ	طِبَّ
قَوِيٍّ	قَوِيٌّ	قَوِيًّا	قَوِيَّ
حَقٍّ	حَقٌّ	حَقًّا	حَقَّ
حُبٍّ	حُبٌّ	حُبًّا	حُبَّ
Practice			
عِزًّا	عَفُوًّا	مَرِدٍّ	حَفِيٌّ
جَمًّا	عَرَبِيٌّ	شَكٍّ	وَلِيٌّ
نَجِيًّا	حِلٌّ	دَكًّا	دَعًا
قَوِيٍّ	حُبٌّ	شَرًّا	حِلٌّ
وَتُحِبُّونَ الْمَالَ حُبًّا جَمًّا		بَلَى وَعَدًا عَلَيْهِ حَقًّا	
يَوْمَ يُدَعُّونَ إِلَى نَارِ جَهَنَّمَ دَعًّا			

Lesson 6 — Waqf (Stopping)

In this lesson, we will be looking at Waqf (stopping) on a letter with a Shaddah (sign of emphasis) or stopping on a round Hā. Be mindful not to skip the Qalqalah or Hams when stopping on a letter in which these characteristics found.

		(ط) Stopping on Tashdīd	
		Practice	
وَتَبَّ ط	وَتَبَّ	لَكُم عَدُوّ ط	لَكُم عَدُوّ
وَلَـٰكِنّ ط	وَلَـٰكِنَّ	أَينَ ٱلۡمَفَرُ ط	أَينَ ٱلۡمَفَرُّ
وَلِيّ ط	وَلِيّ	أَحَقُّ ط	أَحَقُّ
حَجّ ط	حَجُّ	فَجّ ط	فَجّ

		(ط) Stopping on the round Hā	
		Practice	
خَيرًا يَّرَهۡ ط	خَيرًا يَّرَهۥ	وَٱمرَأَتُهۡ ط	وَٱمرَأَتُهۥ
شَرًّا يَّرَهۡ ط	شَرًّا يَّرَهۥ	أَخلَدَهۡ ط	أَخلَدَهۥ
نَادِيَهۡ ط	نَادِيَهۥ	مَوَازِينُهۡ ط	مَوَازِينُهۥ
رَبَّهۡ ط	رَبَّهۥ	مَاهِيَهۡ ط	مَاهِيَهۥ

In this lesson, we will be looking at how to stop whilst reciting a word ending with a round Ta.

• Each letter should be repeated after the tutor, ensuring the learner differentiates between the sounds. This can be achieved by a short pause between each letter.

Stopping on the round Ta			
Practice			
حَسَنَهْ ط	حَسَنَةٍ	بِقُوَّهْ ط	بِقُوَّةٍ
مَا ٱلْقَارِعَهْ ط	مَا ٱلْقَارِعَةُ	مُؤْصَدَهْ ط	مُؤْصَدَةٌ
حَامِيَهْ ط	حَامِيَةٌ	هَاوِيَهْ ط	هَاوِيَةٌ
قَيِّمَهْ ط	قَيِّمَةٌ	مُطَهَّرَهْ ط	مُطَهَّرَةً
Practice			
حَتَّى تَأْتِيَهُمُ ٱلْبَيِّنَةُ ط		نَاصِيَةٍ كَاذِبَةٍ خَاطِئَةٍ ط	
وَ يُقِيمُوا ٱلصَّلٰوةَ ط		سَنَدْعُ ٱلزَّبَانِيَةَ ط	
وَ يُؤْتُوا ٱلزَّكٰوةَ ط		أَوْ مِسْكِينًا ذَا مَتْرَبَةٍ ط	
وَ ذٰلِكَ دِينُ ٱلْقَيِّمَةِ ط		وَ تَوَاصَوْا بِٱلْمَرْحَمَةِ ط	

In this lesson we will be looking at how to stop on a word with a Tanwīn.

- Each letter should be repeated after the teacher, making sure the learner differentiates between the sounds, this can be achieved by a short pause between each letter.

Stopping on a Tanwīn			
	Practice		
زَاهِقْ ط	زَاهِقٌ	عَابِدْ ط	عَابِدٌ
حَرَجْ ط	حَرَجٌ	شَاكِرْ ط	شَاكِرٌ
كَادِحْ ط	كَادِحٌ	أُمَمْ ط	أُمَمٌ
حِجَابْ ط	حِجَابٍ	ثَابِتْ ط	ثَابِتٌ
Practice			
وَ وَضَعْنَا عَنْكَ وِزْرَكَ ط		اَلَمْ نَشْرَحْ لَكَ صَدْرَكَ ط	
وَ طُورِ سِينِينَ ط		وَ ٱلتِّينِ وَ ٱلزَّيْتُونْ ط	
اِقْرَأْ بِٱسْمِ رَبِّكَ ٱلَّذِى خَلَقَ ط		وَ هٰذَا ٱلْبَلَدِ ٱلْأَمِينِ ط	
اِقْرَأْ وَ رَبُّكَ ٱلْأَكْرَمُ ط		خَلَقَ ٱلْإِنْسَانَ مِنْ عَلَقٍ ط	

Stopping on a fathah followed by a Yā	

Practice

رَبِّكَ ٱلْأَعْلَى	رَبِّكَ ٱلْأَعْلَى ط	إِلَّا ٱلْأَشْقَى	إِلَّا ٱلْأَشْقَى ط

وَسَيُجَنَّبُهَا ٱلْأَتْقَى	وَسَيُجَنَّبُهَا ٱلْأَتْقَى ط

Stopping with a madd letter	

Practice

إِنَّكَ أَنْتَ ٱلْعَزِيزُ ٱلْحَكِيمُ	إِنَّكَ أَنْتَ ٱلْعَزِيزُ ٱلْحَكِيمُ ط

مُؤْمِنُونَ	مُؤْمِنُونَ ط	وَلَكِنَّ	وَلَكِنَّ ط

يَوْمُ ٱلدِّينِ	يَوْمُ ٱلدِّينِ ط	لَحَفِظِينَ	لَحَفِظِينَ ط

ثُمَّ إِنَّهُمْ لَصَالُوا ٱلْجَحِيمِ	ثُمَّ إِنَّهُمْ لَصَالُوا ٱلْجَحِيمِ ط

لِيَوْمٍ عَظِيمٍ	لِيَوْمٍ عَظِيمٍ ط

فِرْعَوْنَ وَثَمُودَ	فِرْعَوْنَ وَثَمُودُ ط

Revision 5.6

Remember to continue reciting without spelling and differentiating the sound between the full and empty mouth, short and long letters clearly.

قُلْ أَعُوذُ بِرَبِّ ٱلنَّاسِ	اِنَّكَ أَنْتَ ٱلْعَزِيزُ ٱلْحَكِيمُ
سَيَصْلَىٰ نَارًا ذَاتَ لَهَبٍ	قُلْ أَعُوذُ بِرَبِّ ٱلْفَلَقِ
ثُمَّ إِنَّهُمْ لَصَالُوا ٱلْجَحِيمِ	فِى جِيدِهَا حَبْلٌ مِّن مَّسَدٍ
فَسَبِّحْ بِحَمْدِ رَبِّكَ وَ ٱسْتَغْفِرْهُ	فِى دِينِ ٱللّٰهِ أَفْوَاجًا
لَكُمْ دِينُكُمْ وَ لِىَ دِينِ	إِنَّهُ كَانَ تَوَّابًا
إِنَّ شَانِئَكَ هُوَ ٱلْأَبْتَرُ	فَصَلِّ لِرَبِّكَ وَ ٱنْحَرْ
لِإِيلَٰفِ قُرَيْشٍ	وَ يَمْنَعُونَ ٱلْمَاعُونَ
وَ ٱلْعَصْرِ	إِنَّهَا عَلَيْهِم مُّؤْصَدَةٌ
مَا ٱلْقَارِعَةُ	ٱلْقَارِعَةُ

Silent letters that are written but not recited			
Practice			
وَٱلۡجِبَالَ	لِيُرَوۡا	يَدۡعُوا	فَذُوقُوۡا
تَرۡدٰى	يَخۡشٰى	صَلٰوةٌ	بِٱلۡوَادِ
لِلطَّٰغِينَ	لِلذِّكۡرِ	نَادٰهُ	أَدۡرٰىكَ
إِذَا ٱلشَّمۡسُ	وَٱلصَّيۡفِ	بَنَٰهَا	لِلرَّحۡمٰنِ
فِيهَا ٱلۡفَسَادَ	فِى ٱلصُّدُورِ	أُوۡتُوا۟ٱلۡكِتَابَ	إِذَا ٱكۡتَالُوا
بِٱسۡمِ	بَلۡ تُؤۡثِرُونَ ٱلۡحَيَوٰةَ ٱلدُّنۡيَا		ٱلَّذِى
ذِى ٱلۡأَوۡتَادِ	وَيُقِيمُوا ٱلصَّلَوٰةَ		
وَإِذَا ٱلۡجِبَالُ سُيِّرَتۡ	ذُو ٱلۡفَضۡلِ		
إِلَّا ٱلَّذِينَ ءَامَنُوا وَ عَمِلُوا۟ ٱلصَّٰلِحٰتِ			
فَأَمَّا ٱلۡإِنۡسَانُ	ذُو ٱلۡعَرۡشِ ٱلۡمَجِيدُ		
فَذۡكُرُوا۟ ٱسۡمَ	يُؤۡتُوا۟ ٱلزَّكَوٰةَ		
لَا تَأۡكُلُوا۟ ٱلرِّبَوٰا	وَتَوَاصَوۡا بِٱلصَّبۡرِ		

Revision 5.7

Remember to continue reciting without spelling and differentiating the sound between the full and empty mouth, short and long letters clearly.

فَلْيَعْبُدُوا رَبَّ هٰذَا ٱلْبَيْتِ	وَٱتَّبِعُوهُ لَعَلَّكُمْ تَهْتَدُونَ
أُبَلِّغُكُمْ رِسَالَاتِ رَبِّى	لَنَكُونَنَّ مِنَ ٱلشَّاكِرِينَ
وَلَا يُحَرِّمُونَ مَا حَرَّمَ ٱللَّهُ وَرَسُولُهُ	قُلْ أَعُوذُ بِرَبِّ ٱلنَّاسِ
يُسَبِّحْنَ بِٱلْعَشِيِّ وَٱلْإِشْرَاقِ	مَلِكِ ٱلنَّاسِ إِلٰهِ ٱلنَّاسِ
وَفِى ٱلرِّقَابِ وَٱلْغَارِمِينَ	مِنْ شَرِّ ٱلْوَسْوَاسِ ٱلْخَنَّاسِ
يُجَادِلُونَكَ فِى ٱلْحَقِّ بَعْدَمَا تَبَيَّنَ	ٱلَّذِى يُوَسْوِسُ فِى صُدُورِ ٱلنَّاسِ
ءَامَنَّا بِرَبِّ ٱلْعَالَمِينَ	مِنَ ٱلْجِنَّةِ وَٱلنَّاسِ
رَبَّنَا ٱغْفِرْ لِى وَلِوَالِدَىَّ	فَصَلِّ لِرَبِّكَ وَٱنْحَرْ
ٱلَّذِينَ يَلْمِزُونَ ٱلْمُطَّوِّعِينَ	ذٰلِكَ ٱلَّذِى يَدُعُّ ٱلْيَتِيمَ
مُكِبِّينَ تُعَلِّمُونَهُنَّ	أَلَمْ تَرَ كَيْفَ فَعَلَ رَبُّكَ بِأَصْحَٰبِ ٱلْفِيلِ

Exercise

Word Search

سَ	لَٰ	مَ	مَ	تَ	خَ	ا	فَ	ا
شَ	هِ	ىْ	دَ	أَ	تَ	تَ	لَ	ـٰ
يٰ	زَ	يٰ	زَ	حَ	قَ	سَ	زَ	ـٰ
طِ	ا	طِ	ا	ا	ا	ا	ا	ـٰ
ىْ	رَ	يٰ	زَ	دِ	رَ	لَ	رَ	لَ
نَ	نِ	طِ	ا	ىْ	بَ	هَ	نِ	طِ
وَ	سِ	ىْ	قَ	ثَ	ا	ا	ىْ	ىْ
وَ	ا	رَ	دَ	طَ	ا	لَ	بَ	فَ

سَلَٰمَ	لَطِيْفَ
طَالَبَ	أَحَادِيْثَ
وَارَدَ	شَيٰطِيْنَ
تَخَافَا	شَهِيْدَ
تَقَارَبَا	وَسِيْقَ
تَسَالَهَا	زَارَنِى

رِ	ضْ	وَ	ا	نَ	زِ	ىْ	نَ	لٰ
عِ	زِ	ىْ	نَ	هِۦ	عَ	شِ	ىْ	بِ
سَ	عَ	شِ	ىْ	رَ	تَ	كَ	لٰ	ثِ
هِ	فَ	رِ	ىْ	قَ	ا	نِ	لٰ	ىْ
ىْ	صُ	حُ	فِ	فَ	كِ	هِ	ىْ	نَ
لَ	هِۦ	أَ	لٰ	كُ	لٰ	زِ	ىْ	نَ
ةَ	لٰ	هِۦ	خِ	لِ	لٰ	عَ	شِ	ىْ
عِ	بَ	ا	دِ	ى	سَ	بِ	ىْ	لَ

رِضْوَانَ	عِبَادِى
لٰبِثِيْنَ	فَكِهِيْنَ
سَبِيْلَ	سَهِيْلَةَ
عِزِيْنَ	كُلِى
أَخِى	فَرِيْقَانِ
صُحُفِ	عَشِيْرَتَكَ

Exercise
Word Search

لِ	تِ	ئ	بَ	لُ	اَ	بَّ	بُّ	طِ	
ىَ	وُ	حَ	ئ	بَ	لُ	اَ	بَّ	بُّ	طِبٌّ / طِبّ
وُ	قِّ	ئ	بَ	لُ	اَ	قَ	اَ	بُّ	قَوِيٌّ / قَوِيٍّ
مِ	لُ	اَ	بِ	قَ	قَ	اَ	حُ		حَقٌّ / حَقٍّ
بُّ	اَ	ىًّ	وِ	قَ	قَ	حُ	بَّ	خُ	حُبٌّ / حُبٍّ
بُّ	اَ	يِّ	بَّ	حُ	بِ	بُّ	س		بِالْحَقِّ / خُسْرٍ
قِّ	حَ	لُ	اَ	بِ	قًّ	حَ	رِ		الْبَيْتِ / لِيَوْمٍ
بُّ	بُّ	لُ	اَ	بِ	ئ	بَ	لُ	اَ	

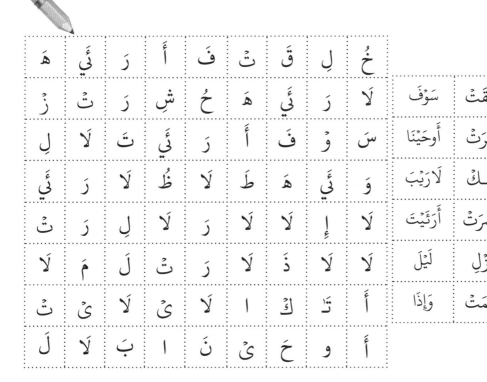

هَ	رَئَي	أَ	فَ	تْ	قَ	لِ	خُ	
زْ	تُ	رَ	شٍ	حُ	هَ	رَئَي	لَا	خُلِقَتْ / سَوْفَ
لِ	لَا	تَ	رَئَي	أَ	فَ	وْ	سَ	فَطَرَتْ / أَوْحَيْنَا
رَئَي	رَ	لَا	ظُ	لَا	طَ	هَ	رَئَي	أَتَـٰكَ / لَارَيْبَ
تْ	رَ	لِ	لَا	رَ	لَا	إِ	لَا	حُشِرَتْ / أَرَئَيْتَ
لَا	مَ	لَ	ثُ	رَ	لَا	ذَ	لَا	هَزْلٍ / لَيْلَ
ثُ	لَا	ىُ	لَا	ا	اِكٰ	تَٰ	أَ	ظُلِمَتْ / وَإِذَا
لَ	لَا	بَ	ا	نَ	ئ	حَ	و	أَ

163

darulqurra.org

القاعدة السمنودية للمبتدئين

Chapter Six

Rules of Nūn & Mīm Sākinah
& the types of Madd

In this lesson, we will be learning the first rule of Nūn Sākinah, called Iẓhār.

- Iẓhār literally means to make something clear.

- When Nūn Sākinah or a Tanwīn precedes one of the throat letters, the Nūn Sākinah or Tanwīn should be recited short, sharp and clear without Ghunnah (nasalisation).

Four rules of Nūn Sakinah & Tanwīn				
Iẓhār				
كُفُوًا أَحَدُ	عَينٍ ءَانِيَةٍ	وَيَنْئَوُنَ	مَنْ ءَامَنَ	ء
سَلَمٌ هِيَ	وَنُوحًا هَدَيْنَا	عَنْهُ	تَنْهَرْ	هـ
فِى جَنَّةٍ عَالِيَةٍ	وَلَيَالٍ عَشْرٍ	مِنْ عَلَقٍ	أَنْعَمْتَ	ع
نَارًا حَامِيَةً	غَفُورٌ حَلِيمٌ	لِمَنْ حَارَبَ	وَٱنْحَرْ	ح
أَمْوَٰتٌ غَيْرُ	مُحْصَنَٰتٍ غَيْرَ	قَوْلًا غَيْرَ	فَسَيُنْغِضُونَ	غ
ذَرَّةٍ خَيْرًا	لَطِيفٌ خَبِيرٌ	لِمَنْ خَشِىَ	وَٱلْمُنْخَنِقَةُ	خ

In this lesson, we will be learning the second rule of Nūn Sākinah, called Idghām.

- Idghām literally means to assimilate or merge.

- When Nūn Sākinah or a Tanwīn precedes any of the Yarmalūn letters, the Nūn Sākinah or Tanwīn will be merged into the Yarmalūn letter

Four rules of Nūn Sakinah & Tanwīn			
Idghām with Ghunnah			
لِقَوْمٍ يَّعْقِلُونَ	يَوْمًا يَّجْعَلُ	أَمَّن يُّجِيبُ	مَن يَّقُولُ	ي
يَوْمَئِذٍ نَّاضِرَةٌ	خَيْرٌ نُّزُلًا	إِن نَّفَعَتِ ٱلذِّكْرَىٰ	مَن نَّشَآءُ	ن
وَظِلٍّ مَّمْدُودٍ	كِتَٰبًا مُّؤَجَّلًا	مِن مَّحِيصٍ	وَمَن مَّعَهُ	م
مَالًا وَّوَلَدًا	مَالٌ وَّلَا بَنُونَ	مِن وَلِيٍّ وَّلَا نَصِيرٍ	مِن وَاقٍ	و
Idghām without Ghunnah			
مَالًا لَّبَدًا	وَمُلْكٍ لَّا يَبْلَىٰ	يُبَيِّن لَّنَا مَاهِىَ	وَمَن لَّمْ	ل
مَثَلًا رَّجُلَيْنِ	شَىْءٍ رَّحْمَةً	وَلَٰكِن رَّحْمَةً	مَن رَّحِمَ	ر

Lesson 3   Rule of Iqlāb

In this lesson, we will be learning the last two rules of Nūn Sākina, called Iqlāb & Ikhfāh.

- Iqlāb literally means to turn

- When Nūn Sākinah or a Tanwīn precedes letter Ba, the Nūn Sākinah or Tanwīn will turn into a Mīm and recited with a Ghunnah.

Four rules of Nūn Sakina & Tanwīn				
Iqlāb				
أَنۢبِيَآءَ	مَسۡحًا بِالسُّوقِ	مُنۢبَثًّا	مِنۢ بَعۡدِ	ب

Lesson 4   Rule of Ikhfāh

- Ikhfā literally means to hide or conceal

- When Nūn Sākinah or a Tanwīn precedes any of the remaining 15 letters of the alphabet, the Nūn Sākinah or Tanwīn will not be recited as clearly like Iẓhār or totally hidden like Idghām

- Ikhfāh is always performed without Ghunnah.

Ikhfāh

أَنْصَارُ ٱللهِ	مَنْصُورًا	فَٱنْصَبْ	ص
فَأَنْذَرْتُكُمْ	وَمِنْ ذُرِّيَّتِي	تُنْذِرُهُمْ	ذ
مَنْثُورًا	سَبْحَتٍ ثَيِّبْتٍ	مِنْ ثَمَرَةٍ	ث
مَلَكٌ كَرِيمٌ	نَاصِيَةٍ كَاذِبَةٍ	لِمَنْ كَانَ	ك
عَيْنٌ جَارِيَةٌ	تُنْجِيكُمْ	مَنْ جَآءَ	ج
مِنْ شَجَرٍ	فَمَنْ شَآءَ	مِنْ شَىْءٍ	ش
سَمِيعٌ قَرِيبٌ	يَنْقَلِبُ	مِنْ قَبْلُ	ق
خَمْسَةٌ سَادِسُهُمْ	خَلَقَ ٱلْإِنْسَانَ	عَبْدَتٍ سَبْحَتٍ	س
مِنْ دُونِ ٱلنَّاسِ	وَكَأْسًا دِهَاقًا	عِنْدَكَ بَيْتًا	د
قَوْمًا طُغِينَ	مُؤْمِنْتٍ قُنِتٍ	إِنْ طَلَّقَكُنَّ	ط
وَلَايُنْزِلُونَ	غُلُمًا زَكِيًّا	أَنْزَلَ	ز
يَتِيمًا فَئَاوَى	مِنْ فَضْلِ ٱللهِ	مُنْفَكِّينَ	ف
إِنْ كُنْتُمْ	تِجَارَةٍ تُنْجِيكُمْ	قُنِتٍ تَبِّتٍ	ت
قِسْمَةٌ ضِيزَى	عَنْ ضَلَّلَتِهِم	مَكَانًا ضَيِّقًا	ض
أَفَلَا يَنْظُرُونَ	مِنْ ظَهِيرٍ	قُرَى ظَهِرَةً	ظ

169

Lesson 5　　Ikhfāh Shafawy & Idghām

In this lesson, we will be learning the first two rules of Mīm Sākinah, called Ikhfāh Shafawy & Idghām.

- Ikhfāh Shafawy literally means to hide or conceal with lips.

- When Mīm Sākinah precedes the letter Ba in a seperate word, the Mīm Sākinah sound will be orally hiden and the lips will be shaped ready to pronounce the letter Ba with Ghunna.

Three rules of Mīm Sakinah				
Ikhfā Shafawy				
أَمْ بِظَٰهِرٍ	لَكُمْ بَرَآءَةٌ	وَهُمْ بَدَءُوكُمْ	رَبُّهُمْ بِذَنْبِهِمْ	ب

- Idghām literally means to assimilate or merge.

- When Mīm Sākinah precedes another vowelised Mīm, then the first Mīm Sākinah will be assimilated into the second vowelised Mīm and recited with Ghunnah.

Idghām			
وَءَامَنَهُم مِّنْ خَوْفٍ	لَهُم مَّغْفِرَةٌ	وَهُم مُّهْتَدُونَ	م

In this lesson, we will be learning the last rule of Nūn Sākinah, called Iẓhār Shafawy.

• Iẓhār Shafawy literally means to make clear with lips.

• When Mīm Sākinah precedes any of the remaining 25 letters of the alphabet (excluding Ba of Ikhfāh, Mīm of Idghām and the letter Alif), then the Mīm Sākina will be pronounced clearly without Ghunnah.

Three rules of Mīm Sakinah			
Iẓhār Shafawy			
فَلَهُمْ أَجْرٌ	بِذَنْبِهِمْ فَسَوّٰىهَا	عَلَيْهِمْ رَبُّهُمْ	فَدَمْدَمَ
كَيْدَهُمْ فِى تَضْلِيلٍ	عَنْهُمْ وَرَضُوا	مَا لَمْ يَعْلَمْ	Remaining Letters
فَجَعَلَهُمْ كَعَصْفٍ	هُمْ يُرَآءُونَ	عَلَيْهِمْ طَيْرًا	
لَكُمْ دِينُكُمْ وَلِىَ دِينِ	وَّامْرَاَتَهٗ	لَمْ يَلِدْ	

Tajweed - Name of Allāh جَلَّ جَلَالَهُ			
Tafkhīm - Full mouth Lām			
تَا ٱللّٰهِ	وَجْهُ ٱللّٰهُ	هُوَ ٱللّٰهُ	ٱللّٰهُ
رَسُولُ ٱللّٰهِ	يَدُ ٱللّٰهِ	عَبْدُ ٱللّٰهِ	يَعْلَمُ ٱللّٰهُ
Tarqīq - Empty mouth Lām			
يُطِعِ ٱللّٰهَ	يَعْصِ ٱللّٰهَ	بِا ٱللّٰهِ	بِسْمِ ٱللّٰهِ
سَبِيلِ ٱللّٰهِ	ذِكْرِ ٱللّٰهِ	بِإِذْنِ ٱللّٰهِ	دُونِ ٱللّٰهِ

Practice			
ذِكْرِ ٱللّٰهِ	وَجْهُ ٱللّٰهُ	نَصْرُ ٱللّٰهِ	يُطِعِ ٱللّٰهَ
رَسُولُ ٱللّٰهِ	بِٱللّٰهِ ٱلْعَزِيزِ	عَبْدُ ٱللّٰهِ	وَٱللّٰهُ أَعْلَمُ
عِبَادُ ٱللّٰهِ	يَعْصِ ٱللّٰهَ	بِا ٱللّٰهِ	هُوَ ٱللّٰهُ
فِي سَبِيلِ ٱللّٰهِ	إِنَّ ٱللّٰهَ	بِإِذْنِ ٱللّٰهِ	دُونِ ٱللّٰهِ
يَعْلَمُ ٱللّٰهُ	تَا ٱللّٰهِ	ٱللّٰهُ	عِنْدَ ٱللّٰهِ
بِسْمِ ٱللّٰهِ	أَنَّ ٱللّٰهَ	وَ ٱللّٰهُ	يَدُ ٱللّٰهِ

Tajweed			

Tafkhīm - Full mouth Rā

لَاتَعذِرُواْ	كَفَرُواْ	نُورُ	رَبُّ
مَا يُؤمَرُونَ	أَمَرَهُم	أَلَم تَرَكَيفَ	نُورَنَا
أَمرُ ٱللَّهِ	مَرُّواْ	بُشرٰى	ذَرَّةٍ
عَلَمَ ٱلقُرءَاَن	رُدَّت	مَرَجَ	مَقدُورًا ۝
وَحُمرُ ۝	بِٱلصَّبرِ ۝	وَٱلوَترِ ۝	وَٱلفَجرِ ۝
وَبَرَزُواْ لِلَّهِ ٱلوَاحِدِ ٱلقَهَّارِ ۝		إِلَى ٱلعَزِيزِ ٱلغَفَّارِ ۝	
لَاتَعذِرُواْ	كَفَرُواْ	مَعَ ٱلعُسرِ ۝	لَفِى خُسرٍ ۝
بُرهَانٌ	ذٰلِكَ مِن عَزمِ ٱلأُمُورِ ۝		مَريَمَ
رَبِّ ٱرحَمهُمَا	لَبِٱلمِرصَادِ	مَنِ ٱرتَضٰى	فِرقَةٍ
لَخَبِيرُ ۝	بِٱلخَيرِ ۝	لَانَصِيرٍ ۝	قِرطَاسٍ

Tarqīq - Empty mouth Rā

قَرِيبًا	يُرِيدُ	أَمرِنَا	مَرِيجٍ
مِن شَـرِّ مَاخَلَقَ		مِن شَـرِّ ٱلوَسوَاسِ	
فِرعَونَ ۝	أَنذِر	وَٱلمَغرِبِ	يُوَدَّ ٱلجرِمُ
لِذِى حِجرٍ ۝	شِرعَةً ۝	يَغفِرلَكُم ۝	مِريَةٍ ۝
إِلَّاٱلنَّذِيرُ	إِلَّاٱلسِّحرُ	وَلَابِكرٌ	ذِى ٱلذِّكرِ

173

المد الواجب المتصل			
The compulsory Attached Madd with a Hamzah in *the same word*.			
أُوْلَـٰٓئِكَ	هَآؤُمُ	جَآءَتْهُمْ	حُنَفَآءَ
وَرَآءَ	مَآءً	سَآئِلٌ	خَطِيٓئَتُهُ

المد الجائز المنفصل			
The permissible Detached Madd from the Hamzah, in *a seperate word*.			
لَمْ يَلْبَثُوٓا۟ إِلَّا	إِنِّىٓ ءَانَسْتُ	وَمَآ أُمِرُوٓا۟ إِلَّا	إِذَآ أَصَبَتْهُمْ
فِىٓ أَحْسَنِ تَقْوِيمٍ		وَمَآ أَدْرَىٰكَ مَا ٱلْعَقَبَةُ	

مد الصلة الصغرى والكبرى		
The Connecting Madd Short & Long used only when *connecting two words*.		
لَهُ مُلْكُ	لَهُۥ مُلْكُ	الصغرى
يُضِلُّ بِهِ كَثِيرًا	يُضِلُّ بِهِۦ كَثِيرًا	الصغرى
وَلَهُ أَسْلَمَ	وَلَهُۥٓ أَسْلَمَ	الكبرى
دُونِهِ أَوْلِيَآءَ	دُونِهِۦٓ أَوْلِيَآءَ	الكبرى

مد البدل ومد العوض		
Madd Badal (Subtituted) preseding the Hamzah & Temporary Madd due to Waqf.		
أُوتُوٓا۟	إِيمَـٰنًا	ءَامَنُوٓا۟	البدل
صُبْحًا	حَكِيمًا	سَوَآءً	العوض

المد العارض للسكون

Temporary Madd due to a temporary Sakūn upon the Waqf letter.

نَسْتَعِينُ	إِلٰهِ ٱلنَّاسُ	هٰذَا ٱلبَيتِ	فِي تَضْلِيلٍ

المد اللازم الكلمى المثقل و المخفف

Madd with a perminent Sakūn in single word, all read heavy except one.

وَلَا ٱلضَّالِّينَ	أَتُحَٰجُّونِّي	تَأْمُرُونِّي	حَاجَّ
ءَآلْـَٰٔنَ المخفف Light	دَآبَّةٍ	وَلَا تَحَٰضُّونَ	وَخَلَقَ ٱلجَآنَّ

الحروف المقطعة

Disjointed Letters found in the begining of chapters and read individually.

ق	قَاف	نۤ	نُونْ
صۤ	صَاد	طٰهٰ	طَا هَا
يٰسۤ	يَا سِينْ	الٓمۤ	أَلِف لَام مِّيمْ
الٓمّرٰ	أَلِف لَام مِّيم رَا	الٓمّصۤ	أَلِف لَام مِّيم صَاد
طٰسٓمّ	طَا سِين مِّيم	طٰسٓ	طَا سِينْ
حٰمۤ	حَا مِيم	حٰمۤ عٓسٓقۤ	حَا مِيم عَين سِين قَاف
كهٰيٰعٓصۤ	كَاف هَا يَا عَين صَاد	الٓمّ ٱللهُ	أَلِف لَام مِّيم ٱللهُ

مۤ 2 or 6 Haraka length

Exercise
Word Search

								وَجَدَ	فُتِحَ
ا	بَ	حَا	ب	صُ	أَ	دَ	جَ	وَ	
ا	ءُ	آ	مَ	تُ	رَ	صِ	نُ	ثُ	نُصِرَتْ / إِيمَٰنًا
ا	ا	ث	نَا	مُ	ى	إِ	ل	اُ	صُبْحًا / ٱلنَّاسُ
تُ	حُ	ا	سُ	ا	نَّ	ل	اُ	تُ	مَآءَ / هَآؤُمْ
ا	تُ	سَ	نَ	ءَا	مُ	ؤُ	آ	هَ	أُوْلَٰٓئِكَ / ءَانَسْتُ
نَ	ا	دُ	طَ	ا	أَ	مُ	ا	ج	جَا / أَحْسَنٍ
ا	سُ	تِ	كَ	كَ	ئِ	لَٰ	وْ	أُ	
حَ	تِ	فُ	يَ	ا	نِ	سَ	حْ	أَ	

								حَآجَّ	دَآبَّةٍ
حَ	بَ	رِ	سُ	خُ	هِ	لَّ	ل	اُ	
آ	عَ	فَ	سَ	لُ	ا	ا	اُ	بِ	حَكِيمًا / نُونْ
جَّ	نُ	ا	ةَ	نَـ	بَ	ا	اُ	ا	عَنْهُ / وَرَآءَ
حَ	هُـ	ا	كَ	و	دَ	لُ	ا	أُ	يَا / ٱللهِ
كِ	ءَ	آ	رَ	وَ	خَ	أَ	بَ	و	أُوتُوا / بِٱلْخَيْرِ
ى	ا	نُ	طَ	ى	خَ	ثُ	مَ	ا	خُسْرٍ / بَنَٰهَا
مَّا	و	تِ	رِ	ا	و	صِ	ا	مُ	
نْ	ىَ	رِ	يَ	أُ	ةٍ	بَّ	آ	دَ	

Revision 6.1

Remember to continue reciting without spelling and differentiating the sound between the full and empty mouth, short and long letters clearly.

خَطِيٓئَتُهُ	دَآبَّةٍ	أُو۟لَـٰٓئِكَ	ءَآلۡـَٔـٰنَ
إِلَـٰهِ ٱلنَّاسِ	لَهُۥ مُلۡكُ	حَآجَّ	سَوَآءٌ
وَلَهُۥٓ أَسۡلَمَ	وَلَا ٱلضَّآلِّينَ	حَكِيمًا	الٓمٓ ۝ ٱللّٰهُ
۝ نٓ	قٓ ۝	وَلَهُۥٓ أَسۡلَمَ	ءَامَنُوا۟
وَرَآءَ	إِيمَٰنًا	تَأۡمُرُوٓنِّىٓ	فِى تَضۡلِيلٍ
وَلَهُۥٓ أَسۡلَمَ	أُوتُوا۟	الٓمٓصٓ ۝	إِنِّىٓ ءَانَسۡتُ
هَآؤُمُ	مَآءً	إِذَآ أَصَٰبَتۡهُمۡ	إِلَـٰهِ ٱلنَّاسِ
أُمِرُوٓا۟ إِلَّا	حٰمٓ ۝ عٓسٓقٓ وَمَآ	صُبۡحًا	لَمۡ يَلۡبَثُوٓا۟ إِلَّا
كٓهيعٓصٓ ۝	هَـٰذَا ٱلۡبَيۡتِ	وَمَآ أَدۡرَىٰكَ مَا ٱلۡعَقَبَةُ	
	فِىٓ أَحۡسَنِ تَقۡوِيمٍ	أُو۟لَـٰٓئِكَ	طسٓمٓ ۝

Exercise
Word Search

									Words	
ا	نَّ	إِ	ب	صُ	ى	لَ	بْ	ثُ		
نَ	و	ضُّ	حْ	تَ	ا	لَ	وَ	ثُ	عَمَّ	ءَامَنُوا۟
ى	لْ	عَ	نُ	ل	اً	ءَ	ل	اَ	كَيفَ	تُبۡلَى
وا	لُ	رْ	أُ	ا	ل	اَ	نَ	اَ	مِن	أُرۡسِلُوا
سِ	ثُ	سَ	نَ	مَ	مُ	كَ	ش	دَ	عَلَى	وَلَاتَحۡضُّونَ
مْ	ا	دُ	نُ	ا	ى	طًّا	ا	ذَ	إِنَّ	دَافِقٍ
ن	سُ	و	تِ	فَ	رَ	فِ	ا	عَ	ذَاتِ	نَشۡطًا
ا	أْ	فُ	يَ	ا	قٍ	تِ	مَّ	أَ		

									Words	
اَ	لِّ	ظِ	وَ	رُ	حْ	سِ	ل	مَ		
رُ	عَ	فَ	مُ	كُ	ي	دِ	رِ		مَرِيج	ءَآلۡـَٔنَ
تَ	ا	نَ	رَ	وُ	نُ	ا	ى		سِحۡرُ	ارۡتَضَى
ضُ	هُـ	ا	كَ	ثًا	بَ	نْ	مُ	جِ	دِينُكُم	نُورَنَا
ى	ءَ	آ	رَ	بْ	لِ	نْ	ىَ		مُنۢبَثًّا	يَنقَلِبُ
ئ	رَ	كُ	ذِّ	ل	اَ	ثُ	مَ	ا	وَمُلۡكٍ	ٱلذِّكۡرَىٰ
مًّا	سُ	تِ	ئَ	دَ	لِ	وَ	لِ	وَ	وَظِلٍّ	وَلِوَلِدَىَّ
كِ	لُ	مُ	نَ	وَ	ءَ	لْ	آ	ءَ		

Revision 6.2

Remember to continue reciting without spelling and differentiating the sound between the full and empty mouth, short and long letters clearly.

لَا أُقْسِمُ بِيَوْمِ ٱلْقِيَمَةِ	وَ ٱلسَّمَآءِ ذَاتِ ٱلْبُرُوجِ
وَ لَآ أُقْسِمُ بِٱلنَّفْسِ ٱللَّوَّامَةِ	وَ ٱلْيَوْمِ ٱلْمَوْعُودِ
بَلَى قُدِرِينَ عَلَى أَن نُّسَوِّىَ بَنَانَهُ	وَ ٱلسَّمَآءِ وَ ٱلطَّارِقِ
إِنَّ عَلَيْنَا جَمْعَهُ وَ قُرْءَانَهُ	خُلِقَ مِن مَّآءٍ دَافِقٍ
مُتَّكِئِينَ فِيهَا عَلَى ٱلْأَرَآئِكِ	عَلَى ٱلْأَرَآئِكِ يَنظُرُونَ
عَمَّ يَتَسَآءَلُونَ	يَوْمَ تُبْلَى ٱلسَّرَآئِرُ
وَ ٱلنَّٰزِعَٰتِ غَرْقًا	إِنَّ إِلَيْنَآ إِيَابَهُمْ
وَّ ٱلنَّٰشِطَٰتِ نَشْطًا	وَ مَآ أُرْسِلُوا عَلَيْهِمْ حَٰفِظِينَ
وَ إِذَا ٱلْمَوْءُدَةُ سُئِلَتْ	وَ إِلَى ٱلسَّمَآءِ كَيْفَ رُفِعَتْ
إِذَا ٱلسَّمَآءُ ٱنفَطَرَتْ	وَ إِذَا رَأَوْهُمْ قَالُوٓا إِنَّ هَٰٓؤُلَآءِ لَضَآلُّونَ

٧

Puzzle 1

								أَعُوذُ	ٱلنَّاس
يُ	صُ	فَا	فِ	ذُ	وَ	عُ	أ	ءَا	
وَ	دُ	گَا	نَ	لُ	لَ	لِ	لُ	ل	مَلِكِ	إِلَهِ
سْ	و	مُّ	بِ	مِ	ءَ	وَ	ءَ	نَّ	ٱلْوَسْوَاسِ	ٱلْخَنَّاس
وِ	رِ	نُ	خُّ	ل	س	لُ	لَّ	ا	ٱلَّذِى	يُوَسْوِسُ
سُ	ظَ	ذُّ	ج	وَ	خَ	مِ	ذِ	سِ	فِى	صُدُورِ
ا	ءَا	نَّ	ا	نَّ	شَا	لِ	ى	فُ	مِنَ	ٱلْجِنَّةِ
لَ	ةِ	سِ	ا	زُ	ا	لِ	ن	ثُ		
سَ	ي	سِ	ى	فِ	ذِ	هِ	لَ	إِ		

Puzzle 2

								قُلْ	بِرَبِّ
مِ	قَ	لَ	خَ	ا	مَ	ى	فِ	ءَا	
نْ	بَ	قَ	وَ	ذِ	هِ	لَ	ل	لُ	ٱلْفَلَقِ	مِنْ شَرِّ
شَ	تٍ	دَ	سَ	ا	نَّ	نَّا	فَ	لُ	غَاسِقٍ	مَا خَلَقَ
رّ	هِ	لَ	إِ	ذَ	فَّ	حَ	ا	لَ	وَقَبَ	ٱلنَّفَّٰثَٰتِ
لُ	بْ	ا	إِ	ا	هِ	لَ	إِ	ق	حَاسِدٍ	ٱلْعُقَدِ
سُ	رَ	نِ	ثَ	حُ	دِ	سِ	ا	حَ	إِذَا	حَسَدَ
قُ	بِّ	ا	حَ	ا	قٍ	سِ	ا	غَ		
لُ	تٍ	حَ	ا	دِ	قَ	عُ	لُ	ءَا		

Grid 1

لُ	قُ	رَ	هُ	لَّ	ل	اَ	لَ	و
هُ	لَّ	ل	اَ	وَ	هُ	ل	وَ	هُ
كُ	ذْ	لِ	يَ	مْ	لَ	صَّ	لَ	ا
فُ	تَ	نْ	كُ	يَ	بَ	مَ	مْ	تَ
وَا	كُ	ذْ	لِ	يَ	مْ	دُ	لَ	و
لَ	و	ذْ	لَ	و	يُ	مْ	لَ	وَ
لَ	و	يُ	هُ	كُ	ذْ	لِ	يَ	مْ
وَ	هُ	خَ	دُّ	حَ	أ	طَ	ل	قُ

Word list:

قُلْ	هُوَ
اَللّٰهُ	هُوَ اللّٰهُ
اَلصَّمَدُ	لَمْ يَلِدْ
وَلَمْ يُولَدْ	وَلَمْ
يَكُنْ	لَهُ
كُفُوًا	اَحَدٌ

Grid 2

لُّ	بْ	حَ	وَ	دِ	سَ	مَّ	ن	مِ
مَ	تَ	اَ	اَ	لُ	حَ	طَ	بَ	لَّا
آ	نَ	اَ	مْ	حَ	طَ	بَ	اَ	تَ
اَ	ا	اَ	رَ	آ	دَ	يَ	اَ	بَّ
غْ	ى	بْ	اَ	اَ	حَ	طَ	بَ	ثْ
نْ	بَّا	تٍ	تُ	ىٰ	لَ	صْ	يَ	سَ
ى	بْ	سُّ	هُ	هًّا	بِ	هَ	لَ	ؤُ
تَبَّ	تَ	وَ	بَ	سَ	كَ	ا	مَ	وَ

Word list:

تَبَّتْ	يَدَآ
اَبِى	لَهَبٍ
وَتَبَّ	مَآ اَغْنٰى
وَمَاكَسَبَ	سَيَصْلٰى
وَامْرَاَتُهُ	اَلْحَطَبِ
حَبْلٌ	مِن مَّسَدٍ

Exercise
Word Search

ب	هِ	لُّ	ل	اَ	نِ	ي	دِ	إِ
حَ	تَ	يْ	أ	رَ	وَ	بَا	ذَا	بَا
مْ	بَا	هُ	لُّ	ل	اَ	رُ	صْ	نَ
دِ	ءَ	آ	جَ	حُ	لْ	تَ	حُ	لْ
رَ	بَا	خْ	بَّ	سَ	فَ	هُ	نَّ	إِ
بِّ	ا	وَّ	تَ	حُ	ثْ	نَ	ا	كَ
كَ	بَا	ا	وَّ	تَ	حُ	تَ	حُ	لْ
بَا	هُ	رُ	فِ	غْ	تَ	سْ	اَ	وَ

إِذَا	جَآءَ
نَصْرُ اللهِ	وَالْفَتْحُ
وَرَأَيْتَ	دِينِ اللهِ
فَسَبِّحْ	وَاسْتَغْفِرْهُ
بِحَمْدِ رَبِّكَ	إِنَّهُ
كَانَ	تَوَّابًا

يَ	عَـ	نَ	و	رُ	فِ	كُ	لْ	اَ
آ	بِ	أ	نَ	أ	دُّ	بِ	ا	عَ
أ	دُ	لُ	قُ	مْ	كُ	نُ	ي	دِ
يُّ	و	نِ	ي	دِ	لِ	وَ	عَـ	قُلْ
هَ	نَ	مْ	تُّ	د	بَ	عَ	ا	مَ
ا	عَـ	مْ	تُ	نْ	أ	آ	لَ	وَ
نْ	نَ	و	دُ	بُ	غْ	تَ	ا	مَ
لَ	آ	أ	عْ	بُ	دُ	مْ	كُ	لَ

يَآ أَيُّهَا	اَلْكُفِرُونَ
لَآ أَعْبُدُ	مَاتَعْبُدُونَ
وَلَآ أَنْتُمْ	قُلْ
أَنَا	مَا عَبَدتُّمْ
عَابِدٌ	لَكُمْ
دِينُكُمْ وَلِيَ دِينِ	مَ

Exercise
Word Search

وَ	هُ	إِ	رُ	تَ	بْ	أَ	لْ	ٱ		
طَ	عُ	نَّ	نْ	كَ	ئِ	نِ	ا	شَ	أَعْطَيْنَٰكَ	إِنَّاۤ
اۤ	لْ	كَ	وْ	ثَ	رَ	طَ	عُ	أَ	فَصَلِّ	ٱلْكَوْثَر
رُ	أُ	لْ	اۤ	طَ	عُ	لِّ	صَ	فَ	وَٱنْحَرْ	لِرَبِّكَ
حَ	نْ	آ	نَّ	إِ	طَ	عُ	طَ	عُ	شَانِئَكَ	إِنَّ
نْ	طَ	عُ	كَ	نْ	يْ	طَ	عُ	أَ	ٱلْأَبْتَرُ	هُوَ
اۤ	طَ	عُ	أَ	أَ	لْ	اۤ	طَ	عُ		
وَ	نْ	طَ	عُ	أَ	كَ	بِّ	رَ	لِ		

صَ	اۤ	نَ	و	عُ	ا	مَ	لْ	اۤ		
بِ	لَ	نَ	لُّ	لُ	يْ	وَ	فَ	لْ	يُكَذِّبُ	عَلَىٰ
اۤ	يُ	ا	و	فَ	دُ	يَ	م		يَدُعُّ	بِٱلدِّين
لْ	كَ	اۤ	تِ	ءُ	فَ	عَ	سْ		وَلَايَحُضُّ	ٱلْيَتِيم
دِّ	ذِ	ذَّ	اۤ	هِ	ا	عُ	لْ	كِ	ٱلْمِسْكِين	فَوَيْلٌ
يَ	بُ	نَ	نَ	اۤ	مَ	رَ	ى	ي	لِلْمُصَلِّين	يُرَاءُونَ
نِ	مَ	ي	تِ	يَ	لْ	اۤ	يُ	نَ	ٱلْمَاعُونَ	صَلَاتِهِمْ
لَّ	مُ	نَ	ي	لَّ	صَ	مُ	لْ	لِ		

183

Exercise
Word Search

ةَ	لَ	خ	رِ	قُ	ى	ذِ	لَّ	اٌ
هَـٰ	وا	اٌ	بَّ	رَ	ذَا	هَـٰ	فَ	ل	قُرَيْشٍ	لِإيلَٰفِ
ذَا	وا	فِ	لْ	يْ	إِ	لِ	لْ	شِّ	رِحْلَةَ	ٱلَّذِى
اٌ	ذَا	وا	وا	شٍ	ذَا	هَـٰ	يَ	تَ	وَٱلصَّيْفِ	ٱلشِّتَاءِ
لْ	فِ	يْ	صَ	ل	اٌ	وَ	عْ	ا	فَلْيَعْبُدُوا	رَبَّ
بَ	مْ	هُ	مَ	عَ	طْ	أَ	بُ	ءِ	هَـٰذَا ٱلْبَيْتِ	أَطْعَمَهُم
يْ	م	هُ	نَ	مَ	ءَا	وَ	دُ	ذَا	مِنْ خَوْفٍ	وَءَامَنَهُم
تِ	اٌ	فِ	و	خَ	نْ	مِ	وا	هَـٰ		

فِ	فَ	رًا	خ	لِ	ي	فِ	لُ	اٌ
فِ	لِ	ي	جِّ	سِ	ن	مِ	كَ	رًا	بِأَصْحَٰبِ	أَلَمْ تَرَكَيفَ
ؤُ	وَ	خ	كَ	زَ	رًا	يْ	بِ	ٱلْفِيلِ	كَيْدَهُمْ
لِ	هُ	هُ	عَ	رَ	رًا	يْ	دَ	خ	طَيْرًا	فِى تَضْلِيلٍ
و	هُ	صً	رًا	تَ	طَـ	هُ	صْ	مِن سِجِّيلٍ	فَجَعَلَهُمْ
كُ	فِ	صً	رًا	تَ	مْ	مَ	أَ	كَعَصْفٍ	مَأْكُولٍ
أُ	مْ	هُ	لَ	جَ	فَ	لَ	بِ		
مَ	لِ	ي	لِ	ضْ	تَ	ي	فِ	أَ		

@DARULQURRAIRC

Join us for more...

حَدَّثَنَا هَنَّادٌ حَدَّثَنَا أَبُو مُعَاوِيَةَ عَنِ ابْنِ أَبِي لَيْلَى وَحَدَّثَنَا سُفْيَانُ بْنُ وَكِيعٍ
حَدَّثَنَا حُمَيْدُ بْنُ عَبْدِ الرَّحْمَنِ الرُّؤَاسِيُّ عَنِ ابْنِ أَبِي لَيْلَى عَنْ عَطِيَّةَ عَنْ أَبِي سَعِيدٍ قَالَ
قَالَ رَسُولُ اللَّهِ ﷺ

مَنْ لَمْ يَشْكُرِ النَّاسَ لَمْ يَشْكُرِ اللَّهَ

وَفِي الْبَابِ عَنْ أَبِي هُرَيْرَةَ وَالأَشْعَثِ بْنِ قَيْسٍ وَالنُّعْمَانِ بْنِ بَشِيرٍ . قَالَ أَبُو عِيسَى هَذَا حَدِيثٌ حَسَنٌ صَحِيحٌ

Abu Hurairah narrated that the Messenger of Allāh ﷺ said :

"Whoever is not grateful to the people,
he is not grateful to Allāh."

Darul Qurra
& ISLAMIC RESEARCH CENTRE

🐦@DarulQurra   f /DarulQurra

Darul Qurrā' & Islamic Research Centre sincerely appreciates the
continuous assistance and support from Jamia Al Karam, The World
Association for Al-Azhar Graduates (WAAG), Samanudi Publications,
City Law Chambers, Pro Accountancy Luton, Millat Auto Spares LTD
and AA Carpets.

CITY LAW CHAMBERS
SOLICITORS, ADVOCATES & COMMISSIONERS OF OATHS

22 Guildford Street, Luton, Bedfordshire LU1 2NR

PRO ACCOUNTANCY
152a Dunstable Road, Luton, LU1 1EW
www.proaccountancy.co.uk

carpets and furniture
SINCE 1991
12-14 Leagrave Rd, LU4 8HZ

بسم الله الرحمن الرحيم

الحمد لله رب العالمين والصلاة والسلام على المبعوث رحمة للعالمين

الذي قال في حديثه الشريف

قَدْ تَرَكْتُ فِيكُمْ مَا لَنْ تَضِلُّوا بَعْدَهُ إِنِ اعْتَصَمْتُمْ بِهِ، كِتَابَ اللهِ

وقال أيضًا صلى الله عليه واله وسلم

يُقَالُ لِصَاحِبِ الْقُرْآنِ : اقْرَأْ وَارْتَقِ وَرَتِّلْ ، كَمَا كُنْتَ تُرَتِّلُ فِي الدُّنْيَا،

فَإِنَّ مَنْزِلَتَكَ عِنْدَ آخِرِ آيَةٍ تَقْرَؤُهَا

فَاللَّهُمَّ صَلِّ وَسَلِّمْ وبارك على الفاتح لِمَا أُغلِق والخاتِم لِمَا سَبَق نَاصِر الحَقِّ بِالحَقِّ

والهَادِي إلى صِرَاطِكَ المُستَقِيم صلاةً تَنحَلُّ بِها العُقَد وتَنفَرِجُ بِها الكُرَب وتُنَالُ بِهَا الرَّغائِب وتُقضَى بِها الحَوَائِج

ويُستَشفَى الغَمَامُ بِوَجهِهِ الكَرِيمِ وعَلَى آلِهِ حَقَّ قَدرِهِ وَمِقْدَارِهِ العَظِيم

الحمدُ لله الذي تَتِمُّ بِنِعمَتِهِ الصَّالِحَات

ولَقَد اختَتَمتُ اليَومَ كِتَابَةً وشَرحًا القَاعِدَة السَّمَنُودِيَّة (بِيُسرٍ وَلِينٍ) لِلمُبتَدِئِين

أَسأَلُ اللهَ العَظِيم أَن يَنفَعَ بِها طُلَّابَ المُسلِمِين وأَن يُجزِينَا بِها خَيرَ الجَزَاءِ فِي الدُّنيَا والأُخرَة

وأَن يَرزُقَنَا دَائِمًا الإِخلَاص والقَبُول وأَن يَرزُقَنَا تِلاوَةَ القُرءَانِ حَقَّ تِلَاوتِه

وأَن يَرفَعَنَا رِفعَةِ القُرءَانِ وأَن يُكرِمَنَا بِكَرَامَةِ القُرءَانِ وأَن يَرحَمَنَا بِالقُرءَانِ وَيَرحَمَ مَن عَلَّمُونَا

وَيَرحَمَ ءابَآئَنَا وأُمَّهَاتِنَا وأَزوَاجِنَا وذُرِّيَّاتِنَا بِالقُرءَانِ

وأَن يَختِمَ لَنَا حَيَاتَنَا جَمِيعًا بِالقُرءَانِ وَبِالإِيمَانِ وَبِالإِحسَانِ وأَن يَختِمَ لَنَا بِخَاتِمَةِ السَّعَادَةِ أَجمَعِين

وَصَلِّي اللَّهُمَّ عَلَى سَيِّدَنَا مُحَمَّدٍ النَّبِيِّ الأُمِّيِّ وَعَلَى آلِهِ وَصَحْبِهِ أَجمَعِين

والحَمْدُ لِلَّهِ رَبِّ الْعَالَمِينَ

الخادم لكتاب الله

الفقير أبو أدم محمد أخلاق الأزهري

مدرس القران الكريم بدار القراء و مركز بحوث الإسلامية

١٠ ربيع الاول ١٤٤٤ هجري

SCAN ME

darulqurra.org